SpringerBriefs in Economics

SpringerBriefs present concise summaries of cutting-edge research and practical applications across a wide spectrum of fields. Featuring compact volumes of 50 to 125 pages, the series covers a range of content from professional to academic. Typical topics might include:

- A timely report of state-of-the art analytical techniques
- A bridge between new research results, as published in journal articles, and a contextual literature review
- A snapshot of a hot or emerging topic
- An in-depth case study or clinical example
- A presentation of core concepts that students must understand in order to make independent contributions

SpringerBriefs in Economics showcase emerging theory, empirical research, and practical application in microeconomics, macroeconomics, economic policy, public finance, econometrics, regional science, and related fields, from a global author community.

Briefs are characterized by fast, global electronic dissemination, standard publishing contracts, standardized manuscript preparation and formatting guidelines, and expedited production schedules.

Aurelie Charles

Sustainable Earnings in a Resilient Economic System

The Power of Groupthink in Channelling Finance Towards Sustainable Goals

Springer

Aurelie Charles
Centre for Development Studies, Social and Policy Sciences
University of Bath
Bath, UK

ISSN 2191-5504 ISSN 2191-5512 (electronic)
SpringerBriefs in Economics
ISBN 978-3-031-67572-0 ISBN 978-3-031-67573-7 (eBook)
https://doi.org/10.1007/978-3-031-67573-7

This Springer imprint is published by the registered company Springer Nature Switzerland AG
The registered company address is: Gewerbestrasse 11, 6330 Cham, Switzerland

Contents

Introduction to "Sustainable Earnings in a Resilient Economic System: The Power of Groupthink in Channelling Finance Towards Sustainable Goals"

Growing up in the 1980s in France, I had a favourite line from a children's story called "Père Lipopette et Sacripan". I learned it by heart, not knowing much of its meaning: "Ecology is the study of the relationship between the living and its environment", which translates from the French: "L'écologie est l'étude des relations entre les êtres et leur milieu". Little did I know that a few decades later this sentence would become the backbone of this book. In effect, the questions that grew with me over the years are actually how do we first understand the system of relationships among the living before looking at its relationship with its immediate context and in particular how do we understand the way resources flow (or not) between human beings? Such journey took me to study economics, first from a neo-classical perspective in France, followed by a more heterodox perspective in the UK, and then developing a PhD thesis which has been influenced by the work of Daniel Kahneman and Amartya Sen for their contribution to behavioural economics and human development theories, respectively. Fifteen years later, this book represents the overall framing that I used to conduct my research since then.

Since childhood, I have always been fascinated to see the way our actions are often tainted by our upbringing, culture, beliefs and values, which has the tendency to silence slowly our child's voice inside. This is what Chap. 1 is covering: the cognitive process through which decision-making and its resulting actions can depart from the actual experience of life when cognitive biases come in and distract us from this experience. Yet, those cognitive biases then serve as the basis for decision-making. While we experience hundreds of cognitive biases, from risk-aversion to confirmation bias, the book seeks to focus on only one: group bias or "groupthink" leading to herd behaviour. As such, there is limited scope for the wide range of cognitive biases impacting on decision-making, but the focus on group bias remains central to economics and resource allocation. It also takes us back to the classical political economists such as Adam Smith, David Ricardo or even Karl Mark whose unit of analysis, as Ha-Joon Chang pointed out, was at the group level, in terms of "class" for example, rather than individuals.

Group bias allows us to show the systemic impact of power relationships between groups on the ways financial resources flow, which is the focus of Chap. 2. We'll see that context matters in the way group belonging is shaped and evolves over time. For example, in the USA, the socio-economic category of financial occupations has evolved over time in the Current Population Survey, from being categorised within a professional occupation of "technicians" in the 1970s to slowly climbing up the ladder of social status and being accounted as "managerial and financial occupations" from the 1990s onwards. This upgrading in social status and earnings went alongside the process of financialisation we have seen in Western economies since the 1980s where group norms of earning distribution at the occupational, race, ethnicity and gender levels were at the heart of systemic group-based financial accumulation. Such systemic dynamics are difficult to capture because individuals are at the intersection of so many different groups. Empirically, this is why it is difficult to capture rent-seeking behaviour at the group level based on individual earnings. To do so, it requires a methodological switch from individualism to groupism to understand the way resources, and financial resources in particular, flow in a global system of relationships between groups, however defined, from socio-demographics to status-seeking consumer groups in digital algorithms.

How to move from an economic system described by mainstream economics thinking as a set of causal and linear relationships which tend to be free from contextual influence to a systemic view of the world with network relationships, nodes, synergies and trade-off in an economic system geared by power relationships between groups? From Chap. 3 onwards, contemporary economic thinking is therefore integrated by bringing in the work of Elinor Ostrom, Kate Raworth and Marianna Mazzucato, among others. Chapter 3 presents the mindset switch required to understand how a resilient economic system functions with and without group biases, at the micro and macro levels. Chapter 4 then goes on to present a system of sustainable earnings which can be resilient to group bubble effects and flexible enough to ease resource (including financial) flows throughout the system. As we will see throughout the book, this bubbling effect that we often see around financial speculations is the aggregation of group biases from micro to macro vertically, but also horizontally across groups, however defined. Such bubbling effect can sustain themselves in a toxic way for the entire system or be eased into a healthier system.

Are the current patterns of group accumulation sustainable?

Well, it depends on the definition of "sustainability". If sustainability is understood as a self-sustaining process of earning accumulation, then the current tacit rules on group norms are certainly self-sustainable and here to stay. Many examples of group norms exist which illustrate how they can create bubbles of consumption which are ecologically damaging: religious groups, with the example of lamb (Easter) and pine trees (Christmas) consumption in Christian traditions; professional groups, with the example of flying off for a 3-day international conference for policymakers and academics; and cultural groups, with the example of Bonfire night in the UK in November when tonnes of CO_2 are released with outdoor woodburning, etc. Taken out of its context, even the group in question would recognise that it does not make ecological sense.

If "sustainability" is understood as "the pursuit of life" (Dahlmann 2024) as it is in this book, then to the question of whether current financial flows feed into a resilient economic system able to feed the needs of sustaining life on Earth, the answer is negative. There is, however, hope in the way bottom-up initiatives and community-led management of ecosystems have been able to tap into the power of groupthink. The final chapter therefore makes a few propositions on how to improve the fluidity and resilience of financial flows, with and without groupthink, before applying them to the Sustainable Development Goals (SDGs) and cultivating islands of SDG excellence from local to regional, national and global SDG priorities.

The original version of the book was inadvertently published with incorrect copyright holder in the front matter. The updated version of this book can be found at https://doi.org/10.1007/978-3-031-67573-7

Chapter 1
Groupthink in Individual Decision-Making

Abstract This chapter provides an understanding of the relationship between this "gut feeling", the inner sense of personal identity, and the identities attached to the social groups surrounding one's life experience. It shows that social identities bring us closer or make us depart from the inner self in the way individuals make decisions (Sect. 1.2), act upon those decisions (Sect. 1.3) which eventually impact on the allocation of resources in human interactions (Sect. 1.4). Finally, it shows that the market economy and associated revealed preferences in market exchange are just the tip of the iceberg in the way group biases at the psychological level affect the process of resource allocation. Collective biases then aggregate at the macro-level in a non-systemic fashion whereby the aggregation of choices by individuals with multiple identities is unpredictable, unless dominant patterns of group behaviour can be identified and acted upon. Hence, the chapter ends by calling for a widening of the resource allocation spectrum from market to social interactions where the rule of legitimacy over access to resources refer to identity-based entitlement in exchange.

1.1 Introduction: What's This "Gut Feeling" All About?

Gut feeling…. something we all experience but do not necessarily act on. We may make decisions to gain others' approval, social recognition and status. We may do so according to what we have been taught in the process of socialisation, at school for example, watching the cool guys and experiencing a sense of belonging or not whether we feel similar or different from them. The process of socialisation thus subconsciously perpetuates norms of behaviour in the collective mind with its savoir-vivre (or not!). Yet, when reminded of this "gut feeling", this inner intuition that feels right to each of us, we can't stop but think that there is more to life than following the herd. Kahneman et al. (2021) posit that this "gut feeling" is linked to the inner belief that a situation complies to the inner belief systems and associated judgements more than an actual emotion. Thus, the perfect compliance of the individual's value judgements with his or her perception of a situation triggers this "gut

A. Charles, *Sustainable Earnings in a Resilient Economic System*,
SpringerBriefs in Economics, https://doi.org/10.1007/978-3-031-67573-7_1

feeling" at the mental level. This chapter is here about understanding the relationship between this "gut feeling", the inner sense of personal identity, and the identities attached to the social groups around us.

A useful way to look at the extent to which we tie ourselves to different group identity is through the *social identity wheel* below, in Fig. 1.1, which has been developed by the Program on Intergroup Relations and the Spectrum Center at the University of Michigan. I invite you to place the numbers 1 to 5 in order of importance to you in the different categories; it is a simple exercise which triggers a useful inner reflection on where we stand individually in the social spectrum, and what this "gut feeling" tells us on whether such stand feels right or not. Another useful and

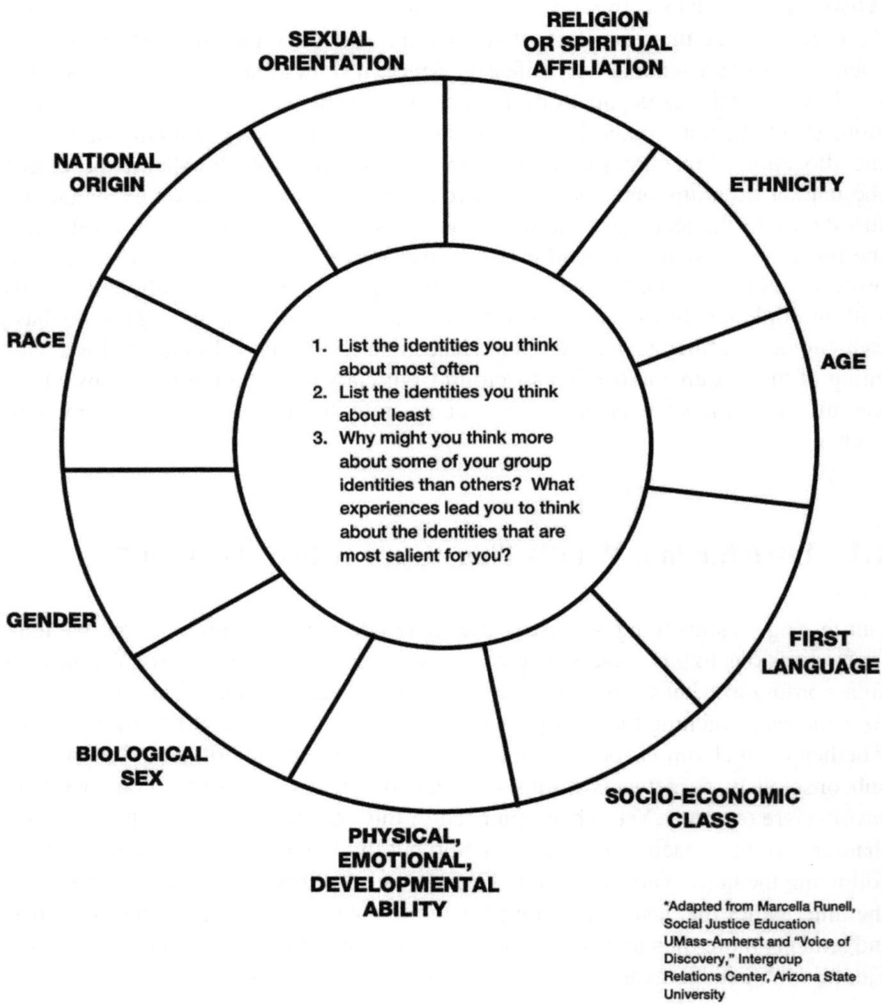

Fig. 1.1 Social identity wheel

subsequent reflection is to recognize that such personal categorisation is not fixed in time, in fact there is a strong probability that doing this simple exercise may lead to different wheels if done now, in 1 year, or 10 years ago… and this is exactly the essence of this chapter, that is to show how social identities bring us closer or make us depart from the inner self in the way individuals make decisions (Sect. 1.2), act upon those decisions (Sect. 1.3) which eventually impact on the allocation of resources in human interactions (Sect. 1.4).

1.2 Groupthink as Cognitive Bias

Ever since the financial crisis of 2008, Western societies have become increasingly divided (Wilkinson & Pickett, 2009, 2019). In such capitalist societies, the balance of power is linked to the financial rewards accumulated by historically dominant groups. Indeed, since the early 1980s when the process of financialisaton took off in Western economies, the human face of capitalism has been represented by managerial white men in finance at the top, and minority groups in low-paid occupations with stagnant real wages, or imprisoned black men at worst, at the bottom of the social stratification (Arestis et al., 2013).

Over the past forty years the exacerbation of wealth and income inequality has had dramatic economic, social, and political consequences. Social norms generate varying wealth and income characteristics associated with different racial groups which has led to the exacerbation of stratified incomes in the US (Arestis et al., 2014). A natural consequence of the rise in inequality is a rise in polarisation of political extremes. In effect, research across 20 advanced countries shows that in the ten years after a financial crisis, far right parties tend to increase their voting share by 30% (Funke et al., 2016). Blame for economic woes is placed at the feet of minority groups which together, in the case of the US, will overtake the share of the White population by 2045 (Frey, 2018).

In 2021, despite the Black Lives Matter movement, the reality of the stratified society in the US is that black and white groups still pray in different churches, live in different neighbourhoods, and have unequal access to health, education and job opportunities (Darity, 2005). The work of Darity, Stewart, Hamilton (2015) and others in the field of stratification economics has well documented those facts thanks to the existence of demographic data in the US statistical platforms (for example the Current Population Survey). However, in other post-colonial countries such as France or Italy, ethnic and racial data is not collected and do not figure in national statistical bodies—the consequence of which is that it keeps the problem of racial and ethnic inequality invisible and is symptomatic of the systemic way discriminatory behaviour reproduces itself in unconscious ways through individual and collective action.

Individual choices influenced by group biases are aggregated in the collective mind which in turn can overtake individual choices. It can be seen in the way social movements gather momentum such as the #metoo or Black Lives Matter movement, or in the way political voices tap into people's fears and emotions to gather momentum, or in the way peer comparison impact on consumption choices. There are in effect many ways in which groupthink can influence the decision-making process of individuals, and not simply in terms of stereotypes. With a world fundamentally uncertain, it is easier to call upon the perceived boundaries of group membership, such as skin colour, gender roles, accents, body shapes, citizenship, religion, occupation or social status gained through consumption or income accumulation, all to rest in a sense of false security and belonging to a social fabric external to oneself. Hence the main issue question raised here is the extent to which individual actions are influenced by a sense of belonging to different social groups. In other words, how much of an individual's decision comes from group memberships and how much comes from the "true"[1] self?

1.2.1 Group Biases and Subjective Wellbeing

Across the disciplines of social sciences, psychology and neuroscience, there is strong evidence that group membership can exacerbate the effect of unconscious biases on individual action (Kahneman et al., 2021). Through MRI brain scans, Kahneman's research has shown that the utility experienced at time t accurately reflects the affect of that moment, the so-called "experienced utility". Kahneman and Krueger's work (2006) have investigated the difference between the affect an individual experiences at time t-1, experienced utility, and the way individuals remember this affect at time t, the so-called "remembered utility". The time difference between the two leads to a systematic bias of perception, which is linked to numerous cognitive biases. This in turn leads to a cognitive dissonance in making decisions since decision-making is based on remembered rather than experienced utility. The action resulting from those decisions therefore bears the cognitive dissonance and departs from the point of affect at time t-1 to include errors linked to cognitive biases. The list of cognitive biases is extensive, from egocentric and anchoring biases to confirmation and gender biases. In the case of group membership for example, norms that are socially ascribed to group characteristics and learned through the process of socialisation are integrated to form a cognitive bias. Such judgement serves as a basis for decision-making at time t, thus overtaking the information gathered with the affect occurring at time t-1. In effect, when reflecting on this experience at time t, cognitive biases kick in and affect the memory of the experience at time. As a result, since decision-making is based on remembered utility, membership of a group will reproduce and exacerbate the group characteristics in human interactions, including market exchange.

[1]The "true" self refers here to the gut feeling mentioned in introduction but we'll see in Chap. 3 how it refers to the self making decisions based on experienced rather than remembered utility.

Such group bias is influenced by peer-comparison and social conditioning in past experiences involving the different social groups to which individuals belong and self-define as 'peers'. This means that there is an element of others' choices in the individual utility function. In the behaviour economics literature, this is called "interdependent preferences" (Gasper & Van Staveren, 2003; Rader, 1980) and relate the fact that one's preferences are related to another's preferences if they identify to each other through peer-comparison. In addition to the impact of interdependent preferences on decision-making, adaptive preferences explain how aspirations change overtime as people tend to get used to what they have, thus putting a higher value on their endowments at time t than at time t-1. In psychology, this notion relates to the fact that individuals experience the so-called "endowment effect" (Huck et al., 2005) or "treadmill effect" (Kahneman & Tversky, 2000).

Figure 1.2 shows how time affects the decision-making process, and within that process how group bias affects individual decisions and actions. At first, life is experienced at time t-1, where sensations interact with the immediate environment or life circumstances. Then independent and adaptive preferences come in to affect the memory of that experience. This is where social conditioning, socialisation, and peer-comparison bias that memory. Decisions tainted by cognitive biases affect remembered utility at time t which is however the point at which a decision is taken and acted upon.

At the point of remembered utility, implicit discrimination is acted upon (Bertrand et al., 2005), whereby unconscious mental association between a target (e.g. African-American) and a given attribute are taking place, i.e. the cognitive biases mentioned before and again here dozens of connected biases impact the decision making process. To understand the extent to which cognitive biases influence individual thinking, Harvard University proposes an interesting Implicit Association Test exploring a range of biases from religious and racial stereotypes to political views and sexual orientation [Take a Test (harvard.edu)]. This test supposedly reveals discrepancies between social attitudes and individual reasoning, which is not without its criticisms. In particular, a critique is pointing out that the test tends

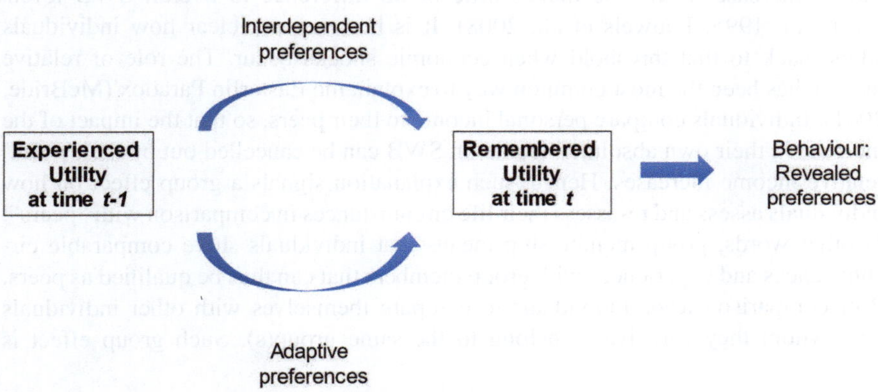

Fig. 1.2 How do cognitive biases affect behaviour over time?

to gear the mind towards common knowledge, irrespective of whether or not the participant endorses these social attitudes (Arkes & Tetlock, 2004). Nevertheless, it remains a useful tool to become aware of potential cognitive biases, whether they belong to the collective mind taught through the socialisation process, or to the true self.

1.2.2 External Shocks on Subjective Wellbeing[2]

Unless individuals are brain-scanned at the point of experienced utility, it is practically impossible to observe experienced utility. We can however observe remembered utility through revealed preferences. Hence, the question raised here is how external shocks on life circumstances impact on remembered utility or subjective wellbeing? And what is the role of group membership in adjusting to these external shocks? In effect, given that the external shocks brought about by climate change are affecting the process of resource allocation and consumption on a global scale, the response needs to be at a pace and scale that can match its global outreach. Group bias can accelerate or decelerate the pace and scale of climate policy interventions and hence global decision-making from the bottom-up.

First, let's look at how external shocks impact on Subjective Well-Being (SWB), used as a proxy for remembered utility here. Taking the 2008 financial crisis as an example of an external shock on life circumstances, the behavioural nature of this event is linked to simultaneous housing and financial bubbles related to group behaviour at the bottom and top of the income distribution, respectively. Such event impacted on the SWB threshold of various social groups. The presence of a threshold in relation to SWB came to light with the Easterlin Paradox (Easterlin, 1974, 1995, 2005). In Easterlin's (1995: 35) own words: "within a country at a given time those with higher incomes are, on average, happier. However, raising the incomes of all does not increase the happiness of all", and beyond a certain income level, any further increase in income makes little or no difference to overall SWB levels (Easterlin, 1995; Pouwels et al., 2008). It is however not clear how individuals adjust back to that threshold when economic shocks occur. The role of relative income has been the most common way to explain the Easterlin Paradox (McBride, 2001). Individuals compare personal income to their peers, so that the impact of the increase in their own absolute income on SWB can be cancelled out by their peers' relative income increases. Hence, such explanation signals a group effect on how individuals assess and re-assess their life circumstances in comparison with "peers". In other words, group membership means that individuals share comparable circumstances and experiences with group members that can thus be qualified as peers. Peer comparison leads individuals to compare themselves with other individuals with whom they perceive to belong to the same group(s). Such group effect is

[2] This section draws from Charles et al. (2019).

unconscious and leads to cognitive biases in individual decision-making (Akerlof & Kranton, 2010), as shown for example by Bertrand et al. (2005) with the instance of implicit discrimination.

The literature on group membership shows that group behaviour tends to be more self-centred and predictable than individual behaviour (Bornstein et al., 2004; Charness & Sutter, 2012; Brown & Yang, 2015). In the experimental laboratory setting, Bornstein et al. (2004) provide evidence from experiments with strategic games that group members are more rational in terms of maximising the payoff for each group member, and that they are less pro-social toward other groups. Group players assume that players in other groups behave similarly which triggers a self-reinforcing norm to maximise the group's aspirations for higher payoffs. Outside the laboratory setting, Brown and Yang (2015) show that the relative social value between men and women leads women to be underestimated by the betting system in jump racing, where, as jockeys they can compete equally. In the social setting, group membership strongly affects the individual's perception of life circumstances through peer comparison. As pointed out by Dolan et al. (2008: 105), "perceptions of our circumstances can be very important predictors of life satisfaction". In effect, in their comprehensive literature review of the factors associated with SWB, the word "perception" itself appears six times for six different factors. Hence, since group membership influences the individual's perception of life circumstances, we wonder the extent to which group membership influences SWB.

Second, to understand group membership in SWB, we need to look at how group membership influence individuals' ranking of life domains in SWB. In Charles et al. (2019), we postulate that group membership influences the ranking of the life domains affecting SWB which then allows individuals to go back to their individual threshold. Personal circumstances such as health-related or the loss of relatives will however move individuals away from their individual threshold without a resilient effect (Easterlin, 2005). To assess this proposition, we assess SWB by group and its evolution over time. Most studies in economics and psychology relate to SWB from the point of view of the individual (Diener & Suh, 2000; Kahneman & Tversky, 2000). In most cases, SWB refers to the self-evaluation of people's lives but the way group membership influence self-evaluation is not clear. Kahneman and Krueger's work (2006) helps our understating in that respect since they have been investigating the difference between the affect an individual experiences at time $t - 1$, what is called experienced utility, and the way individuals remember this affect at time t, what is called remembered utility as explained with Fig. 1.2. Kahneman and Krueger (2006) further show that life circumstances have a greater impact on experienced rather than remembered utility which means that external shocks on an individual's subjective well-being will have an impact on experienced utility, which will then be biased by peer comparison at the point of remembered utility. Urry et al. (2004) have also shown that the correlation between remembered utility and brain readings is minimal (around 0.30), which tend to suggest that reporting at time t a level of utility experienced at time $t - 1$ gives an inaccurate picture of experienced utility.

Such findings support the view that investigating self-reported satisfaction levels in different domains of life accurately measure remembered utility biased by peer comparison, and not experienced utility. This is important when considering the impact of a peer or group effect on individual behaviour because individual choice is based on remembered utility rather than experienced utility. At the level of remembered utility, group membership influences individual SWB by affecting the hierarchy of life domains in the SWB function. For example, the dominant norm for self-employed individuals may be to value their job on a higher scale than employed individuals. Here, the argument is not concerned with the heterogeneity versus homogeneity of groups but rather that, since remembered utility is affected by peer comparison, individual perception of life circumstances is influenced by the hierarchy of the life domains of the groups to which they belong. Then, since each individual belongs to multiple groups, the ranking of the life domains should be revealed at the group rather than individual level, and it should also differ according the intersection of groups investigated, for example, a female self-employed plumber versus a male employed plumber. In effect, as pointed out by Crenshaw (1989), the intersectionality of group memberships can lead to different normative outcomes compared with considering groups separately.

Together with peer comparison, adaptation to life circumstances through adaptive preferences or hedonic adaptation has been highlighted as another important factor that will return SWB to its individual threshold (Clark et al., 2005; Clark, 2006; Binder & Coad, 2010, 2011). From the happiness perspective, the "endowment effect" (Huck et al., 2005) or "treadmill effect" Kahneman and Tversky (2000) shows that people have a tendency to get used to life circumstances in the sense that they adapt their perceptions and judgments to get back to their individual threshold. Further evidence of adaptive preferences has been gathered by Burchardt (2005) in the context of constant and increasing incomes, linking the argument to the risk-aversion of individuals. The argument put forward by Rabin (2001) however is that risk aversion is intrinsically linked to utility derived from wealth rather than income. In effect, March (1988) shows that risk aversion and risk-taking behaviour depend on wealth outcomes compared to aspiration levels of wealth. Since housing is a major component of wealth (Campbell & Cocco, 2007), SWB housing factors are expected to affect negatively the SWB setpoint when a house bubble bursts as life circumstances changes the aspiration levels on wealth, at least in the short-run. Other life circumstances such as marriage, serious injuries, death of relatives or job loss also tend to "defect a person above or below this setpoint, but in time hedonic adaptation will return an individual to the initial position" (Easterlin, 2005: 29).

The insight of Easterlin's work that this research is starting from is that attainment in each domain is not the key to happiness, but rather the relative value attached to all domains. In particular, we postulate that this relative value depends on adaptive and interdependent preferences vis-à-vis other group members and between groups. As such, external economic shocks affect the relative value of domains within and across groups as shown in Fig. 1.3. While economic shocks are likely to have an impact on net affect, or experienced utility at time $t - 1$, by affecting life circumstances, it does not necessarily show in life satisfaction figures which are biased by peer comparison. The evidence collected by Dolan et al. (2008: 106) on attitude towards unemployment and inflation by political groups in effect "lend

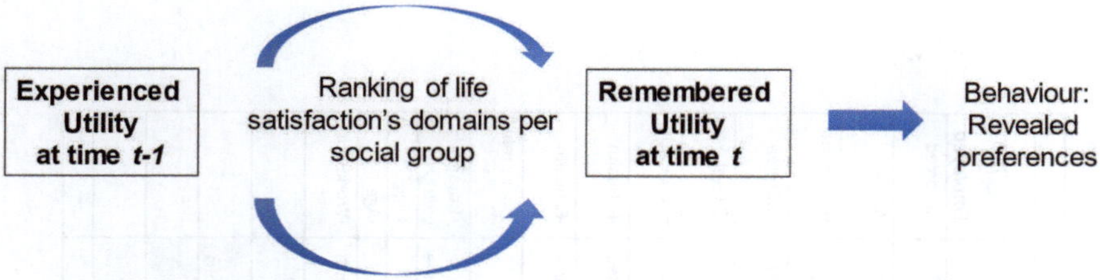

Fig. 1.3 Ranking of life domains per social group and SWB

support to the idea that the impact of external circumstances is dependent upon perceptions and attitudes". Hence, economic shocks that have a group effect component, such as herd behaviour leading to a housing bubble, is likely to influence the bias brought about by peer comparison that affect life satisfaction or remembered utility at time *t*.

To test this hypothesis, using data from the British Household Panel Survey (BHPS) for 1996–2000, and 2002–2008, and from its follow-up data set Understanding Society—UK Household Longitudinal Study (UKHLS) for 2009–2014, we assess the impact of group membership on the ranking of the domains of life-satisfaction. At the group level, SWB will depend on the domain satisfaction as shown in Table 1.1. We use BHPS and UKHLS data from 1996 to 2014 on two professional groups (self-employed and employee) with two layers of group membership (male and female) leading to four different groups, namely male self-employed, female self-employed, male employee, and female employee. As self-reported life-satisfaction data, BHPS and UKHLS is equivalent to remembered utility affected by cognitive biases, experienced utility being impossible to estimate unless with instant MRI scans of the brain. We estimate SWB for each group at three different points in time which reflect remembered utility at three points in time and thus show the evolution of group biases on the ranking of life domains' satisfaction.

Table 1.1 shows the ranking of the different domains classified by the size, in descending order, of the statistically significant coefficients in each group for the three periods. The domains linked to housing have been shaded to highlight the discrepancies in rating prior to and after the 2008 crisis. In effect, the striking element of Table 1.1 is that housing factors have improved in ranking from 1996 to 2008 to end at the top of the classification across groups in 2008 before dropping considerably in the post-2008 period. For example, home ownership was classified from second place for female employees to fourth place for other groups in the period 1996–2000, jumping to the first rank for male employees, all women, and second rank for self-employed men in the period 2002–2008, and then dropping to the tenth place for self-employed women, 13th place for male employees, 16th place for female employees and not being statistically significant for self-employed men. Similarly, the ranking of the variable "problem paying for housing" followed the same trend of home ownership over the entire 1996–2014 period, when we could expect that such variable would become of great significance in the event of

Table 1.1 Classification of significant SWB domain coefficients by size and sign (1996–2014)

	1996-2000				2002-2008				2009-2014			
	Male		Female		Male		Female		Male		Female	
Rank	Employee	Self-Employed	Employee	Self-Employed	Employee	Self-Employed	Employee	Self-Employed	Employee	Self-Employed	Employee	Self-Employed
1	-V.P. Health	+Partn. pay^2	-V.P. Health	-V.P. Health	+House own	-Partn. pay^2	+House own	+House own	-Income^2	+Widowed	-Income^2	+Divorced
2	+Partn. pay^2	+Separated	+House own	-Poor Health	+Exc.Health	+House own	+House rent	+House rent	-P. Health	+Divorced	-P. Health	-A level
3	-P. Health	-V.P. Health	-P. Health	+House rent	+House rent	+House rent	+Exc.Health	+Exc.Health	+Exc.Health	-A level	-Widowed	+Exc.Health
4	+House own	+House own	+House rent	+House own	-Partn. pay^2	+Exc.Health	-V.P. Health	-PbPayHous	-H.degree	-O level	+Divorced	-H.degree
5	+Exc.Health	+House rent	-PbPayHous	-H.degree	-V.P. Health	-PbPayHous	-PbPayHous	+G. Health	+Income	-H.degree	+Exc.Health	-O level
6	+House rent	-PbPayHous	+Exc.Health	-PbPayHous	+G. Health	-V.P. Health	-P. Health	+Age^2	-F. Health	-P. Health	+H.degree	+VG.Health
7	-PbPayHous	+Married	+Married	+Married	-PbPayHous	+G. Health	+G. Health	-Age	+Divorced	+Exc.Health	+Separated	-P. Health
8	+Married	+A level	-Separated	+Exc.Health	-P. Health	-Poor Health	+Married	+Partner pay	-FirstDegree	+Separated	+Married	-F. Health
9	+O level	+Exc.Health	+Age^2	-Partner pay^2	+Married	+O level	-Partn. pay^2		+V.G. Health	+Married	-A level	-House rent
10	+Divorced	-Poor Health	-Partn. pay^2	-A level	-Income^2	+A level	-Income^2		+Married	-FirstDegree	-FirstDegree	+House own
11	-Income^2	+O level	+G. Health	+Age^2	+Divorced	+Married	+A level		-O level	+VG.Health	-F. Health	+Age^2
12	+Age^2	+Age^2	-Age	+Partner pay	-Separated	+Income	+Age^2		-A level	-F. Health	-O level	-Age
13	+A level	-Age		-Age	+A level	+Partner pay	-Age		+House own	-PbPayHous	+VG.Health	-WorkHour
14	+G. Health	+Partner pay			+Age^2	-Age	+Partner pay		+Age^2	-House rent	+Income	
15	+Income	+ WorkHour			-Age	+ WorkHour	+O level		-Age	+Age^2	-PbPayHous	
16	+Partner pay				+Partner pay		+Income		-PbPayHous	-Age	+House own	
17	-Age				-WorkHour		-WorkHour		-WorkHour	-WorkHour	-House rent	
18	-WorkHour										+Age^2	

Source: Charles et al. (2019)

the Great Recession in the post-2008 era. Instead, in the post-2008 era, we observe a different pattern of ranking by professional group. The first satisfaction domain affecting the SWB of employees is the squared income variable, which means that the prospects of income opportunities and associated rising level of uncertainty linked to the Great Recession negatively affect SWB, whether men or women. Poor level of health is the second domains affecting negatively employees' SWB.

In terms of the ranking of life domains by social group, there is some evidence of a group effect being consistent per group. For example, looking at the domain ranked first after 2008, it differs between the self-employed group as a whole—with family status being the major contributor to SWB, and the employee group as whole—with income stability being the major contributor to SWB. Looking at a gender group effect within the self-employed group, being divorced or separated used to be important for self-employed men in affecting positively SWB prior to 2008, and it has become the first domain for self-employed women too from 2009. Hence, to a certain extent there is a sense that the financial crisis may have reinforced professional group identity. However, the evidence on group effects needs further investigation to unpack the overlap of group memberships in SWB measurement.

The findings suggest a "keeping up with the Joneses" group effect on remembered utility, or life satisfaction, whereby housing domains have steadily increased in importance in influencing SWB up to 2008 before collapsing to the lowest ranks of SWB domains in the post-2008 era. Figure 1.4 illustrates this point whereby external shocks impact on the affect of life circumstances, at the point of experienced utility, which is then processed through a re-ranking of life domains through group membership at the point of remembered utility. Such evidence confirms the presence of peer-comparison in SWB, and it raises the issue of the extent to which the Easterlin paradox could be understood in terms of group comparison and the associated relative value of satisfaction domains within and across groups, however defined.

Now, since cognitive biases affect the decision-making process of an individual, a subsequent question is whether such biases are having a positive or negative impact on interpersonal relationships. In effect, as one cognitive bias, group membership and associated herd-behaviour is essential for making rapid positive behavioural changes, but it can also be a force leading to environmental damages to a

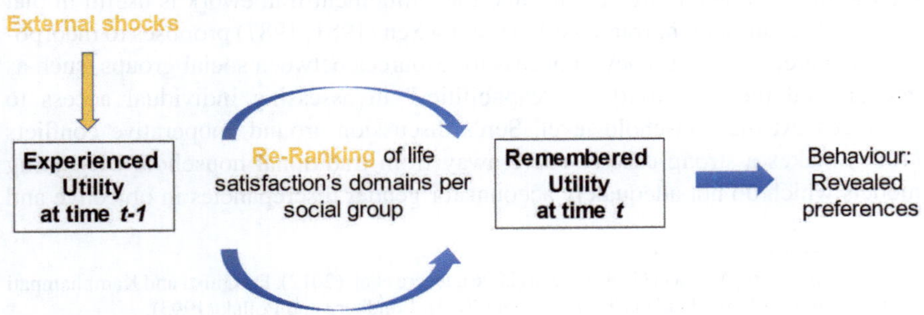

Fig. 1.4 Impact of external shocks on subjective well-being

scale seen from the consumption and production patterns over the course of the Great Acceleration (Steffen et al., 2015). The remaining of the chapter will therefore look at the way group behaviour affects life circumstances; how it changes human interactions and how it impacts on resource allocation starting here at the household level, the first point of socialization.

1.3 Group Behaviour in Human Interactions

The cognitive biases mentioned so far represent a psychological phenomenon which sustains itself over time with significant economic and human costs. As consumers, investors, migrants, professionals, daughters and fathers, inherited and unconscious roles of behaviours affect all daily decisions and impact the most visible aspects of social life. Social and domestic violence, increasing polarisation and inter-group conflicts are also consequences of these cognitive bias (Wilkinson & Pickett, 2019; Stewart, 2008). Hence, understanding how biases are formed and transmitted is important to link the psychological individual roots of decision-making to the social and economic impact of decision-making. Learning to belong to different group identities is part of the socialisation process and with the household being the first point of socialisation, the following section looks at the way social identities and group membership influences one's access to resources at the household level.

While it is well documented in social sciences that social identities and associated norms of behaviour[3] influence an individual's access to resources, it is less clear how social identities affect remembered utility, or "subjective" wellbeing, versus experienced utility, or "objective" wellbeing. The meaning of objective wellbeing here is that the "objective" sensory experience of life a time *t-1* is not subject to cognitive biases, unlike remembered utility at time *t*. Subjective wellbeing is therefore relating here to remembered utility or, in other words, to the perception of the sensory experience subject to cognitive biases. Figure 1.5 below shows that the market economy and associated revealed preferences are just the tip of the iceberg in the way group bias at the psychological level affects resource allocation at the market level.

Both objective and subjective determinants of wellbeing should be included in the framing of human interactions, and the entitlement framework is useful in that respect. The entitlement framework based on Sen (1981, 1987) proposes to incorporate the perceived legitimacy of access to resources between social groups, such as gender, and the objectivity of "capabilities" in assessing individual access to resources. At the household level, Sen's discussion around cooperative conflicts (1987) makes a strong case to move away from traditional household bargaining models which do not adequately account for gender discrepancies in objective and

[3] See, among others, Agarwal (1997), Basu (2006), Deere et al. (2012), De Giusti and Kambhampati (2016), Folbre (1986), Handa (1994), Iversen (2003), Lundberg and Pollak (1993).

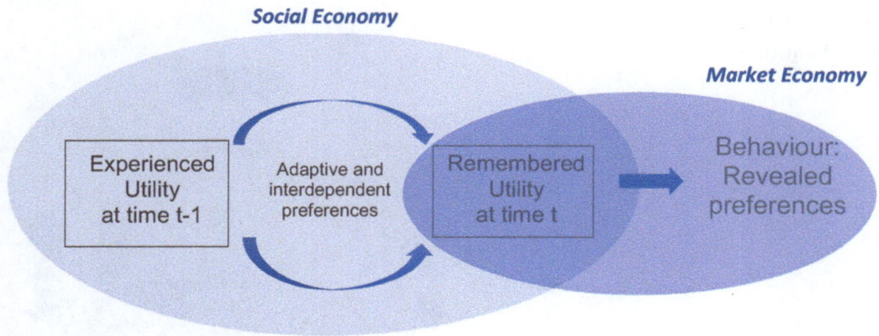

Fig. 1.5 The Market Economy: the tip of the iceberg of the invisible social economy

subjective wellbeing. One of his propositions is to expand the informational basis of the household model with "capabilities" and "functionings" to assess objective wellbeing, while keeping a subjective element in wellbeing assessment with perceived interest of the different parties to account "for the causal influence of perceptions on ideas of propriety and legitimacy of different institutional arrangements and through that on the respective well-beings of men and women" (Sen, 1987: 5). Bargaining models of resource allocation have moved a long way since Becker's view (1965) but the essentialist assumption of men versus women with socially ascribed gender characteristics persists.

The literature in feminist economics has long shown the importance of moving away from essentialist interpretations of gender differences since it tends to reinforce gender stereotypes rather than questioning them (Folbre, 2001; Nelson, 2014; Sent & van Staveren, 2019). In experimental behaviour research, most empirical findings tend to promote an essentialist view of gender differences whereby there is either an explicit ascribed dichotomy between genders (e.g. "women are found to be …") or an implicit dichotomy "through assuming that men and women make free choices based on their respective innate characteristics" (Sent & van Staveren, 2019: 3). Gender is intrinsically relational and such embedment in the organic nature of the social setting makes it difficult to quantify the economic value of the so-called "feminine" or "masculine" traits without apriorist assumptions based on gender stereotyping, especially as such traits tend to differ across cultural settings (Nelson, 2014; Folbre, 2001). The relational aspect of gender is central to the understanding of household relationships as the social construct of "gender" is about being different, not better, being shaped by social relations, over time and space rather than being static (Charles, 2021).

In the context of intra-household resource allocation, the individual identity-based entitlement shown in Fig. 1.6 incorporate two elements. First, the perception of legitimacy or "entitlement" in the household setting (Sen, 1987) is tainted by group biases, including gender, as they set the rules of human interactions and access to resources, within and beyond the household. The perception of legitimacy in Sen (1987) describes how the perceived contributions and interests within the household setting are endogenous to the bargaining process and how they differ

Fig. 1.6 Individual Identity-based entitlement

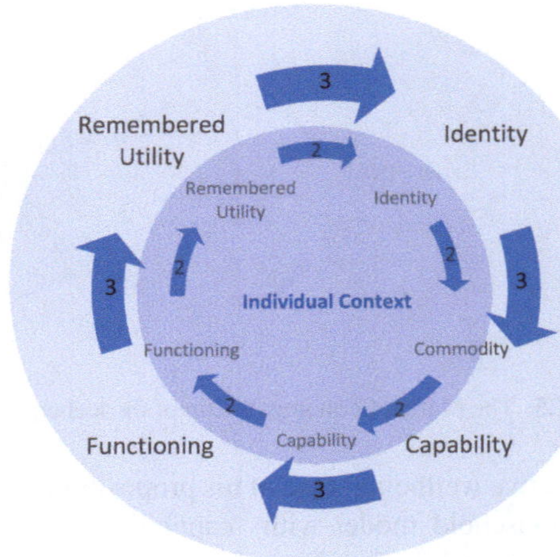

between the parties. Such difference of perception is likely to be context dependent according to different social identities, whether it is in terms of gender, culture or age. This calls for a more fluid definition of "gender" as brought forward by feminist economics in the sense that the perception of gender itself may vary across time and space. Context matters in the way identity is shaped in relation to others, and gender in particular. Such relationality calls for different tacit rules of resource allocation which do not ascribe resources to perceived gender or identity attributes. In turn, different rules of resource allocation, which would be "identity-free" could improve the resilience and flexibility of resource allocation, especially in a context of increasing resource scarcity. It remains to be seen what would serve as a basis for different rules of resources allocation, if any, as will be explored later in the book.

Second, both objective and subjective elements of wellbeing are central to the bargaining process (Sen, 1987). In the breakdown position of cooperative conflict when household members fail to cooperate, the resulting position of each member is dependent on both an objective measure of wellbeing—assessed through capabilities; and a subjective measure reflecting the perceived legitimacy of access to resources between the parties (Sen, 1987). The subjective measure will however be bearing the cognitive biases, including group identity, that serve as a basis for decision-making at the level of remembered utility. Accounting for both objective and subjective wellbeing nonetheless departs from utilitarianism and the use-value of household interactions by incorporating perceptions of legitimacy between members in wellbeing assessment and highlighting its role in shaping capabilities in a context of resource scarcity in particular.

Social norms in effect convey the rules of legitimacy in access to resources between identity groups where group membership is sustained according to certain ideal criteria of behaviour that sustain group membership. Hence, an individual has multiple identities shaped by social interactions, which entitles him or her to a socially acceptable level of resources (Tienda & Lii, 1987; Massey, 2007; Schippers, 2007). Social identities are endogenous to an individual agency and personal identity as it tends to evolve dynamically over time (Davis, 2011). As such, there is a deterministic element of social life that shapes the way individuals access resources, a perceived legitimacy in social exchange, which depends on the position of the individual's salient identity on the spectrum of social stratification (Akerlof & Kranton, 2010; Davis, 2011; Darity, 2005; Grusky, 2019).

With social norms, individuals consider to be entitled to resources according to their social identities, which provide an incentive to sustain the norm that resources should be ascribed to some rather than others. In times of increasing scarcity, the process of resource allocation follows these rules of allocation more than ever. "Entitlement is essentially a legal concept, dealing with rules that govern who can have the use of what." (Sen, 1987: 30) Sen has long worked on "entitlements" and failures of access to resources, the theoretical foundations of which served as a basis for the Capability Approach (Sen, 1999). In particular, he argues that the Bengal famine of 1943 was due to entitlement failures to food supply rather than to a shortage of food supply per se (Sen, 1981). In Sen's writings the concept of entitlement relates to rules of legitimacy between sets of ownerships whereby "an entitlement relation applied to ownership connects one set of ownerships to another through certain rule of legitimacy. It is a recursive relation and the process of connecting can be repeated." (Sen, 1981: 1). Since his framework applies to market interactions, the rule of legitimacy depends on trade-based entitlement, production-based entitlement, own-labour entitlement, and inheritance and transfer entitlement. Hence, given that Sen's approach focuses on market interactions only, the causal link between commodity and utility depends on the individual capability to transform a commodity into utility (Sen, 1999). Thus, the causal link between "commodity" and "utility" is (Clark, 2006):

(1) Commodity ➔ Capability (to function) ➔ Function(ing) ➔ Utility,
instead of the Utilitarian approach: Commodity ➔ Utility.

With an entitlement framework based on societal exchange, the rule of legitimacy extends to identity-based norms of behaviour which is influenced by the power relationships between identity groups. Extending from the social to the market economy as we did in Fig. 1.5, with market exchange being a subset of social exchange, the rule of legitimacy here will refer to identity-based entitlement in exchange, and the causal relationship (1) above becomes a circular relationship with identity-based norms of behaviour bearing group biases through remembered utility, as the rules of legitimacy in market interactions (2):

(2) Identity ➔ Commodity ➔ Capability (to function) ➔ Function(ing) ➔ Remembered Utility ➔ Identity;

which is one identity-based entitlement relation in market exchange, as a subset of social interactions (3);

(3) Identity ➔ Capability (to function) ➔ Function(ing) ➔ Remembered Utility ➔ Identity;

which is one identity-based entitlement relation in social interactions, as shown in Fig. 1.6.

Given that "identity" is a relational concept, if one identity is considered to be entitled to a specific set of resources at the expense of others, irrespective of individual agency, then the outcome of the process of resource allocation will follow the rule of allocation defining the entitlement relationship of this identity. The proposition made here however is that, if there is no socially ascribed rule of resource allocation, then no rule prevails in the process of resource allocation and the rule of identity-based entitlement shown in Fig. 1.6 does not apply. Instead, the prevailing "rule" of allocation is based on experienced utility where scarce resources are shared in a way that maximises the current life expectancy of all. This is consistent with the argument advanced by Jay Winter (1986) and Amartya Sen (1998) that the increased life expectancy of people in England and Wales in the two decades between WWI and WWII was the result of resources being rationed and shared more equally, such as food supply, which in turn maximised the survival of the entire population in the long-run. Based on experienced utility, decision-making places the actual context of resource allocation at the heart of the allocation process. As such, resources themselves and their preservation in particular will be central to social and hence market exchange. Chapter 3 will expand the discussion further on this.

1.4 Time, Space and Identity

We have seen so far that time matters in the way cognitive biases affect our perception of life experiences (at time t), but that cognitive biases do not necessarily affect the experience of life itself (at time t-1) which itself is more affected by changes in life circumstances. Yet, we have seen that decision-making at the individual level is based on that perception rather than on life experience itself. This means that, if one looks at the aggregate level of a country for example, hundreds of individual and collective biases will aggregate at the macro-level in a non-systemic fashion, whereby the aggregation of choices by individuals with multiple identities is unpredictable, unless dominant patterns of group behaviour can be identified and acted upon. This is where the concept of "noise" becomes important to understand the aggregation process. Kahneman et al. (2021) in effect make the distinction between the role of cognitive bias and the role of "noise" in decision-making. While cognitive bias and judgements can be accounted for at the aggregate level, and shows in standard deviations, a strong identity element in individual decision-making do influence decisional outcomes in a non-random fashion. At the aggregate level, individual decisions can have a strong variance in outcomes which can be referred to as "noise". Kahneman et al. (2021) take the example of judges in the US court system who, with a similar set of cases, end up with highly dissimilar judgmental outcomes—with life circumstances such as the time of the day, the mood in the moment, or depending on how sunny the day is, seem to influence the variance in outcomes and hence increasing the noise in the samples collected. On the other hand, when cognitive biases are more dominant than noise on the decision outcome, the decision-maker seems to recall on the perceived boundaries of group membership as criteria of decision-making, i.e. identities and perceived sense of belonging of individuals are called upon as decision criteria. At the macro-level, we will see in the next chapter how individual biases aggregate in the process of financial accumulation and economic exchanges.

The second element strongly impacting on decision-making is space: the individual context in which decision-making is made, at the point of remembered utility, i.e. the context in which decision-making takes place influences its outcome. In effect, an exactly similar decision-making process taking place in two different places can lead to two different outcomes. The context in which decisions are made are also shaped by these cognitive biases in the sense that the salient identity of an individual in a particular context will override other identities in a sort of survival strategy. This is why it is important to understand the construction of identity in one space by mapping out the historical dynamics of power which make some identities more dominant than other in human interactions. The work of Suk-Young Chwe (2013) is insightful in that respect as it shows how people who tended to be undermined in social interactions, due to slavery for example or in the patriarchal context of the characters in Jane Austen's novels, tend to develop higher strategic abilities. Slaves and female characters in respective contexts are able to think a few steps ahead of the game in order to be able to survive according to the rules of the game of social legitimacy dictated by the dominant group. Being able to map out the rules of legitimacy that are context-specific is key to understand the rules of human interactions and financial accumulation, as we will now see in Chap. 2.

Ultimately, identity is a social construct at the intersection of time—how individual's sense of belonging to groups influence one's decision and behaviour; and space—how the aggregation od individual biases are context-specific and affect human interactions in one space to the extent that it biases the perception of life experience. Elaborating on Sen's work on entitlement, we have seen that widening the spectrum from market to social interactions, with market exchange being a subset of social exchange, the rule of legitimacy over access to resources refer to identity-based entitlement in exchange. So the main questions the remaining of the book is exploring are: how does groupthink impact on human interactions over time, over space and across identities? How would an economic system look like if all decisions were based on experienced utility, i.e. free from cognitive biases? Would it be a world geared by the invisible hand of Adam Smith and actual trickle down effects? Or would be a theatre of many more conflicts over resources?

References

Agarwal, B. (1997). "Bargaining" and gender relations: Within and beyond the household. *Feminist Economics, 3*(1), 1–51.

Akerlof, G. A., & Kranton, R. E. (2010). *Identity economics: How our identities shape our work, wages, and well-being*. Princeton University Press.

Arestis, P., Charles, A., & Fontana, G. (2013). Financialisation, the 'Great recession' and the stratification of the US labour market. *Feminist Economics, 19*(3), 152–180.
Arestis, P., Charles, A., & Fontana, G. (2014). Identity economics meets financialisation: Gender, race, and occupational stratification in the us labour market. *Cambridge Journal of Economics, 38*, 1471–1491.
Arkes, H. R., & Tetlock, P. E. (2004). Attributions of implicit prejudice, or Would Jesse Jackson 'Fail' the implicit association test? *Psychological Inquiry, 15*(4), 257–278.
Basu, K. (2006). Gender and say: A model of household behaviour with endogenously-determined balance of power. *The Economic Journal, 116*, 558–580.
Becker, G. S. (1965). A theory of the allocation of time. *The Economic Journal, 75*, 493–517.
Bertrand, M., Chugh, D., & Mullainathan, S. (2005). Implicit discrimination. *The American Economic Review, 95*, 94–98.
Binder, M., & Coad, A. (2010). An examination of the dynamics of well-being and life events using vector autoregressions. *Journal of Economic Behavior and Organization, 76*, 352–371.
Binder, M., & Coad, A. (2011). From average Joe's happiness to miserable Jane and cheerful John. *Journal of Economic Behavior and Organization, 79*, 275–290.
Bornstein, G., Kugler, T., & Ziegelmeyer, A. (2004). Individual and group decisions in the centipede game: Are groups more "rational" players? *Journal of Experimental Social Psychology, 40*, 599–605.
Brown, A., & Yang, F. (2015). Does society underestimate women? Evidence from the performance of female jockeys in horse racing. *Journal of Economic Behavior and Organization, 111*, 106–118.
Burchardt, T. (2005). Are one man's rags another man's riches? Identifying adaptive expectations using panel data. *Social Indicators Research, 74*(1), 57–102.
Campbell, J. Y., & Cocco, J. F. (2007). How do house prices affect consumption? Evidence from micro data. *Journal of Monetary Economics, 54*, 591–621.
Charles, A. (2021). Gender, financial crisis and labor markets. In K. Zimmermann (Ed.), *Handbook of labor, human resources and population economics*. Springer Cham. https://doi.org/10.1007/978-3-319-57365-6_29-1
Charles, A., Wu, D., & Wu, Z. (2019). Economic shocks on subjective well-being: Re-assessing the determinants of life-satisfaction after the 2008 financial crisis. *Journal of Happiness Studies, 20*, 1041–1055. https://doi.org/10.1007/s10902-018-9986-y
Charness, G., & Sutter, M. (2012). Groups make better self-interested decisions. *Journal of Economic Perspectives, 26*, 157–176.
Clark, D. A. (2006). Capability approach. In D. A. Clark (Ed.), *The Elgar companion to development studies*. Edward Elgar.
Clark, A. E., Etilé, F., Postel-Vinay, F., Senik, C., & Van der Straeten, K. (2005). Heterogeneity in reported well-being: Evidence from twelve European countries. *The Economic Journal, 115*, C118–C132.
Crenshaw, K. W. (1989). Demarginalizing the intersection of race and sex: A black feminist critique of anti-discrimination doctrine, feminist theory and antiracist politics. *University of Chicago Legal Forum, 129*, 139–167.
Darity, W. (2005). Stratification economics: The role of intergroup inequality. *Journal of Economics and Finance, 29*, 144–153.
Darity, W., Jr., Hamilton, D., & Stewart, J. (2015). A tour de force in understanding intergroup inequality: An introduction to stratification economics. *Review of Black Political Economy, 42*(1–2), 1–6.
Davis, J. B. (2011). *Individuals and identity in economics*. Cambridge University Press.
De Giusti, G., & Kambhampati, U. S. (2016). Women's work choices in Kenya: The role of social institutions and household gender attitudes. *Feminist Economics, 22*(2), 87–113.
Deere, D. C., Alvarado, G. E., & Twyman, J. (2012). Gender inequality in asset ownership in Latin America: Female owners vs household heads. *Development and Change, 43*(2), 505–530.
Diener, E., & Suh, E. M. (2000). *Culture and subjective well-being*. MIT Press.

Dolan, P., Peasgood, T., & White, M. (2008). Do we really know what makes us happy? A review of the economic literature on the factors associated with subjective well-being. *Journal of Economic Psychology, 29*, 94–122.

Easterlin, R. A. (1974). Does economic growth improve the human lot? Some empirical evidence. In R. David & R. Reder (Eds.), *Nations and households in economic growth: Essays in honor of moses abramovitz*. Academic.

Easterlin, R. A. (1995). Will raising the incomes of all increase the happiness of all? *Journal of Economic Behaviour and Organization, 27*, 35–48.

Easterlin, R. A. (2005). Building a better theory of well-being. In L. Bruni & P. L. Porta (Eds.), *Economics and happiness: Framing the analysis*. Oxford University Press.

Folbre, N. (1986). Hearts and spades: Paradigms of household economics. *World Development, 14*(2), 245–255.

Folbre, N. (2001). *The invisible heart: Economics and family values*. The New Press.

Frey, W. H. (2018). *Diversity explosion: How new racial demograhics are remaking America*. Brookings Institution Press.

Funke, M., Schularick, M., & Trebesch, C. (2016). Going to extremes: Politics after financial crises, 1870-2014. *European Economic Review, 88*, 227–260.

Gasper, D., & Van Staveren, I. (2003). Development as freedom v-v and as what else? *Feminist Economics, 9*(2–3), 137–161.

Grusky, D. (2019). *Social stratification, class, race, and gender in sociological perspective*. Routledge.

Handa, S. (1994). Gender, headship and intrahousehold resource allocation. *World Development, 22*(10), 1535–1547.

Huck, S., Kirchsteiger, G., & Oechssler, J. (2005). Learning to like what you have—Explaining the endowment effect. *The Economic Journal, 115*, 689–702.

Iversen, V. (2003). Intra-household inequality: A challenge for the capability approach? *Feminist Economics, 9*(2–3), 93–115.

Kahneman, D., & Krueger, A. B. (2006). Developments in the measurement of subjective well-being. *Journal of Economic Perspectives, 20*(1), 3–24.

Kahneman, D., & Tversky, A. (2000). *Choices, values and frame*. Cambridge University Press.

Kahneman, D., Sibony, O., & Sunstein, C. R. (2021). *Noise: A flaw in human judgment*. William Collins Books.

Lundberg, S., & Pollak, R. A. (1993). Separate spheres bargaining and the marriage market. *Journal of Political Economy, 101*(6), 988–1010.

March, J. G. (1988). Variable risk preferences and adaptive aspirations. *Journal of Economic Behavior and Organization, 9*(1), 5–24.

Massey, D. S. (2007). *Categorically unequal: The American stratification system*. Russell Sage Foundation New York.

McBride, M. (2001). Relative income effects on subjective well-being in the cross-section. *Journal of Economic Behavior and Organization, 45*, 251–278.

Nelson, J. A. (2014). The power of stereotyping and confirmation bias to overwhelm accurate assessment: The case of economics, gender, and risk aversion. *Journal of Economic Methodology, 21*(3), 211–231.

Pouwels, B., Siegers, J., & Vlasblom, J. D. (2008). Income, working hours, and happiness. *Economics Letters, 99*, 72–74.

Rabin, M. (2001). Diminishing marginal utility of wealth cannot explain risk aversion. In D. Kahneman & A. Tversky (Eds.), *Choices, values and frames*. Cambridge University Press.

Rader, T. (1980). The second theorem of welfare economics when utilities are interdependent. *Journal of Economic Theory, 23*(3), 420–424.

Schippers, M. (2007). Recovering the feminine other: Masculinity, femininity, and gender hegemony. *Theory and Society, 36*(1), 85–102.

Sen, A. (1981). *Poverty and famines: An essay on entitlement and deprivation*. Oxford University Press.

Sen, A. (1987). *Gender and cooperative conflicts*. Working papers, 18, UN Wider.
Sen, A. (1998). Mortality as an indicator of economic success and failure. *The Economic Journal, 108*(446), 1–25.
Sen, A. (1999). *Development as freedom*. Oxford University Press.
Sent, E.-M., & van Staveren, I. (2019). A feminist review of behavioral economic research on gender differences. *Feminist Economics, 25*(2), 1–35.
Steffen, W., Broadgate, W., Deutsch, L., Gaffney, O., & Ludwig, C. (2015). The trajectory of the anthropocene: The great acceleration. *The Anthropocene Review, 2*(1), 81–98. https://doi.org/10.1177/2053019614564785
Stewart, F. (Ed.). (2008). *Horizontal inequalities and conflict: Understanding group violence in multiethnic societies*. Palgrave Macmillan.
Suk-Young Chwe, M. (2013). *Jane Austen*. Princeton University Press.
Tienda, M., & Lii, D. T. (1987). Minority concentration and earnings inequality: Blacks, Hispanics, and Asians compared. *American Journal of Sociology, 93*(1), 141–165.
Urry, H., Nitschke, J., Dolski, I., Jackson, D., Dalton, K., Mueler, C., et al. (2004). Making a life worth living. *Psychological Science, 15*(6), 367–372.
Wilkinson, R. G., & Pickett, K. (2009). *The spirit level: Why equality is better for everyone*. Bloomsbury Press.
Wilkinson, R. G., & Pickett, K. (2019). *The inner level: How more equal societies reduce stress, restore sanity and improve everyone's well-being*. Penguin Book.
Winter, J. (1986). *The great war and the British people*. Springer.

Chapter 2
Group Membership in Capital and Labour Earnings

Abstract This chapter provides evidence of how group biases aggregate in the process of financial accumulation and the way they affect economic exchange over time. What can we learn on group behaviour from the demographics of capital and labour earnings historically, regionally, nationally and across borders? At the national level, what can we learn from the interdependence of earning trends between groups on the social entitlement rules to financial flows? Being able to map out the rules of legitimacy that are context-specific is key to understanding the tacit rules of human interactions and financial accumulation. Looking at the most visible (data-wise) part of the market economy, the relationships between the historical trends of labour and capital earnings are investigated by gender, race, nationality and occupation for the US, UK and France. It shows that there a two-tier economic system where earnings go in the hands of a few dominant groups at the top of the income distribution, while leaving labour earners with stagnant real-wages.

2.1 Keeping up with the Joneses … But Which Ones?

An important factor that has contributed substantially to the 2008 financial crisis and 'Great recession' emerged from the steady but sharp rise in the unequal distribution of income between capital and labour, and within labour among different income groups. For instance, in the US the top 1% of households accounted for only 8.9% of income in 1976, but this share grew to 23.5% of the total income generated before the crisis in the summer of 2007 (Rajan, 2010). It has been suggested that the rise in inequality together with financial liberalisation and innovation have generated the financial crisis, although the mechanisms have differed between the USA (and in part in the UK) and continental EU (Fitoussi & Saraceno, 2010). To understand these mechanisms and the extent to which they differ between the UK and continental Europe, this chapter goes beyond the current literature on income inequality which is looking at the sectoral and industrial income shifts (Galbraith, 2012), or changes in income strata (Atkinson et al., 2011; Milanovic, 2016; Piketty, 2014) to adopt an identity-based approach to income inequality, as I have done in

A. Charles, *Sustainable Earnings in a Resilient Economic System*,
SpringerBriefs in Economics, https://doi.org/10.1007/978-3-031-67573-7_2

the past (Arestis et al., 2013, 2014; Charles, 2011, 2012; Charles et al., 2011), and to financial accumulation in particular. Financial accumulation here is understood as individual earnings from capital (e.g. capital income such as interest or dividends, inheritance, capital gains, and insurance compensation) and labour (e.g. wages and labour income), which is how I refer here to capital and labour earnings.

The elements of groupthink in decision-making described in the previous chapter should show in the patterns of financial accumulation over time. In effect, the "Keeping up with the Joneses" effect has been a triggering factor in enhancing the momentum towards the Great recession, whether it is at the top of managerial and financial occupations with excessive earnings to keep up with the social status of such occupations, or at the bottom of the social ladder where subprime mortgages entertained the dream of feasible access to homeownership for low-income earners. Low-income earners saw homeownership as a possibility because their peers in the group of low-income earners were having access to homeownership. "Keeping up with the Joneses" is a groupthink effect but the issue raised in the previous chapter around the multiple layers of group membership one can identify to leads to the subsequent question: which Joneses? In other words, how do the layers of group membership come out in the dynamics of labour and capital earnings?

This chapter therefore seeks to map out financial flows between social groups in the past in order to show the social entitlement rules to financial flows in the past: what can we learn on group behaviour from the demographics of capital and labour earnings historically, regionally, and nationally? At the national level, what can we learn from the interdependence of earning trends between groups on the social entitlement rules to financial flows? The subsequent question for Chap. 3 will then be: how do past social entitlement rules to financial flows feed into the dynamics of future financial flows?

2.2 Group Behaviour in Financial Accumulation

2.2.1 Financial Accumulation: Individual or Group Phenomenon?[1]

As seen in the previous chapter, the literature distinguishes between group and individual behaviour (Bornstein et al., 2004; Charness & Sutter, 2012; Muehlheusser et al., 2015), whereby norms of behaviour by a social group tend to have an impact on individual decision-making. Similarly, in stratification economics, various authors show how race and ethnic group disparities in market outcomes can be sustained and exacerbated over time (Darity & Williams, 1985; Massey, 2007; Grusky & Weisshaar, 2014; Tienda & Lii, 1987). In effect, the relative economic value socially assigned to groups of individuals is mostly historically determined and

[1] This section draws from Charles and Sguotti (2021).

culturally embedded. Social norms convey the rules of legitimacy for the access to resources between social groups, where group membership is sustained according to certain ideal criteria of behaviour that sustain group membership. An individual belongs to multiple identities that are shaped by social interactions, and each identity socially entitles him or her to a socially acceptable level of resources (Davis, 2011; Akerlof & Kranton, 2010). Social identities are endogenous to an individual's personal identity since they tend to evolve dynamically over time and thus, questions the use of methodological individualism to capture the dynamics of inequality between social groups (Davis, 2011). In effect, there is a deterministic element of social life that shapes the way individuals access resources—a perceived legitimacy in social exchanges, which depends on the position of the individual's identities on the spectrum of context-based social stratification (Davis, 2011; Akerlof & Kranton, 2010; Darity, 2005).

When economic exchange takes place, social norms serve as rules for reproducing the advantages of certain social groups at the expense of others. For instance, in the context of the United States, Arestis et al. (2014) have shown how occupational, race, and gender characteristics are reinforced by the exacerbation of earning differentials between demo-graphic groups during the financialization period of 1980–2010. Another example at the intersection of context and educational elites is the evidence from England and Wales that shows that a large number of employers offering the top-paid jobs in the country target an average of only 19 universities (out of 130) in the United Kingdom for those jobs (Dorling, 2013). These examples go beyond the issue of statistical discrimination since group productivity is not responsible for income inequality across all occupations (Tomaskovic-Devey & Skaggs, 1999). Rather, the problem lies in the combined effect of identities on inequality since the sum of identities can lead to worse discriminating outcomes than when considering identities separately, as argued by the intersectionality literature (hooks, 2015; Crenshaw, 1989; McCall, 2005). Compared with implicit discrimination (Bertrand et al., 2005) or with Becker's taste discrimination, the concept of intersectionality departs from methodological individualism by questioning the boundaries that can be drawn between groups and by defining individuals by a unique combination of diverse groups. As such, it allows us to assess the multiple layers of discrimination over time, one layer of which is gender.

Methodologically, trying to grasp the multiple layers of group belonging over time is challenging. First, using traditional regression methods on individual income or earnings as dependent variable with a range of independent individual variables around education, skills or experience means that the dynamic element will be left in the residuals of the regression. It means that the power dynamics at play over time between groups in access to education, skills or experience will not be visible in the explanatory power of the regression. Instead, as will be presented below with the experience of the US, the UK and France, the method used for each case is based on analysing the trends of group rather than individual earnings. Analysing trends could be done via vector autoregressions (VAR) or cointegration analysis, depending on the nature of the trends. For example, Arestis et al. (2014) conducted cointegration analysis on labour earnings between demographic groups in the US since

1980. Such method allows to reveal the long-term relationship(s) in earnings between demographic groups but it is constrained by the number of data points available for significant results, and such demographic time-series are rarely available across countries and over long time-series.

Second, the power dynamics in the multiple layers of group membership evolves over time in a way that makes it difficult to track empirically. For example, in the Current Population Survey (King et al., 2010), if you track down financial occupations back in time, the currently known "financial" occupations were "technician" occupations in the late 1970s. However, over time, the social status of financial occupations has risen to such an extent over time that they now belong to the top "managerial and financial" occupations. Similarly, another statistical issue is the lack of visibility of group membership which are simply non-existent. For example, collecting race-based data is still taboo in France due to the traumas of WWII. In effect, a 1978 law bans the collection and storage of race-based data which means that no race or ethnic data exists in one of the most multi-cultural societies of the West. A consequence is that problems of discrimination are not statistically visible, which present issues of transparency and accountability in discriminatory practices against racial and ethnic groups.

2.2.2 Group Example: Gender in Financial Accumulation[2]

Over the past forty years, the process of financialization in Western economies has had significant distributional effects on the global income distribution, often reinforcing existing gender inequalities. Fukuda-Parr et al. (2013) demonstrate how such dynamics in income distribution at the macroeconomic level have been reinforced over the past 40 years. Financial institutions and intermediaries have developed financial instruments that enable the expansion of lending in the housing sector and in parts of the household economy that were previously deemed too risky to lend to: "the so-called subprime loans were "predatory" (a term that refers to loans made under unfair, deceptive, or fraudulent conditions in the loan origination process), targeted to people of color and single female heads of households" (2013: 9). Here, for the US experience, the macroeconomic processes of financial liberalization have exacerbated the existing social stratification by race, ethnicity and gender.

From the relational lens on gender, financial crises are intrinsically related to the meaning of "gender" and the consequent crisis of "masculinity" emerging globally as a consequence of financial crises. In effect, Fukuda-Parr et al. (2013) argue that "[t]here is evidence from recent financial crises that, due to norms of masculinity, there is a greater tendency for unemployed men to suffer from shame and inadequacy upon loss of their breadwinning status, so much so that in some countries men's suicide rates rise in periods of crisis" (2013: 23). In the Global North,

---

[2] This section draws from Charles (2021).

financial liberalization meant that investments in physical assets and factories were becoming less attractive than speculative investments in financial markets, i.e. the rate of return on financial capital was more rewarding than investment in traditionally more "masculine" construction and manufacturing sectors. At the global level, such gender norms are also visible in the way financial liberalization, which includes trade liberalization, leads to an expanded use of cheap female wage labour, drawing female labour away from the unpaid household economy to the paid economy—and export-processing zones in particular. When a financial crisis hits the global economy, demand for manufactured goods decreases and threatens the employment of women, generally dominant in export-led industries, representing for instance 85% of labour in the garment industry in Bangladesh, and 85% in cut flowers in Uganda (Walby, 2009). Over time, the pre-existing gender norms are affected by a rebalancing of female bargaining power with previously unemployed women now bringing an income in the household economy, thus challenging the traditional breadwinner model and the ideals of "masculinity" within it.

The model proposed by Elson (2010) in the context of the global crisis post-2008 seeks to map out the socio-economic dynamics at play in the way a financial crisis affects the social bond in labour markets and the household. Elson offers three different rounds of effects in the financial, productive, reproductive spheres and these rounds of effects essentially depend on the gender interactions between the different spheres and the timeframe adopted, short-run and long-run effects. For example, during a crisis, when paid employment and social welfare tend to be cut, there is an increasing need for the unpaid care economy to fill in the relational gaps left by such cuts. Hence, this adds further pressure on the reproduction sphere and strains further the relations between household members, thus affecting the quality of interactions and functioning of the household unit. Similarly to the increase in racism towards minority groups in relation to a dominant group during periods of adverse economic conditions (Vargas et al., 2018), a recession exacerbates the gender relationship of "feminine" versus "masculine" ideals. The impact of the financial shortage damages the social fabric by threatening the ideal of masculinities with increased suicide rates, rising domestic violence, family abandonment by household heads in the reproductive sphere together with a deterioration of employment opportunities for men, and cuts in welfare support for working mum in the productive sphere (Floro & Dymski, 2000; Karamessini & Rubery, 2013). Post-1997, the experience of Asia facing cuts in welfare services put further pressure on the household economy with increasing debts, job losses and declining incomes (Floro & Dymski, 2000). While the social bond was severely affected by a crisis, the strength of the Asian social bond sustained in the reproductive sphere also meant that it acted as a social safety net since many households survived thanks to family and community links.

Across studies, the gendered impact of financial crises on the labour market tends to depend on the quality of the social bond between the three spheres, i.e. depending on how well women's work is embedded in social norms and expectations (Lopez-Andreu & Rubery, 2018). When comparing women's employment trajectories in the UK and Spain during the Great Recession, Lopez-Andreu and Rubery (2018) show that the type of austerity measures and the degree to which they affect the reproductive sphere will subsequently affect the productive sphere, depending on the gender division of labour by occupation and contract type. This echoes similar findings by Peinado and Serrano (2018) who looked at the evolution of gender gaps in employment, earnings and unemployment before and after 2008 in France, the UK, Spain and Italy. Gender norms are here strong drivers of earning and occupational disparities, and such norms have been reinforced by the Great Recession. The overall pattern here is towards the reduction of gender gaps in employment and unemployment but mainly due to worsening outcomes for men in "masculine" occupations such as construction, and an increase in the precarization of employment, such as part-time employment where female labour participation is high. Context-dependency in gender inequality is also described with, for example, high sensitivity to shocks for Spain compared with France, which point out to different gender relationships within the household and the labour market together with country-specific social policies and labour market regulations. Similar findings are found in Karamessini and Rubery (2013) who, across nine case studies, demonstrate that while there was a deterioration in men's employment in the aftermath of the crisis, the austerity policies have more than offset this deterioration with its negative effects on the demand for female labour and for services supporting working mothers. As a consequence, they argue that austerities measures have reinforced "the same failed mechanisms that caused the crisis in the first place and is stalling or even reversing the long-term growth in social investment in support for care." Hence, any policy route that would sensibly address the causes and consequences of a financial crisis should place gender equality at its core.

In non-Western economies, the gendered impact of financial crises on the labour force is also deeply linked to the quality of the social between the three spheres. For example, in the context of the Asian financial crisis of the late 1990s, the impact on the labour market in the Philippines did not necessarily mean higher levels of unemployment for women than men, but it meant longer hours in formal employment and unpaid care employment (Walby, 2009). This is perhaps one of the key points in understanding the gendered impact of financial crisis compared to other social groups present in the labour market; that the overrepresentation of women in the invisible informal and unpaid economy makes it hard to quantify and trace the extent of the damage on women's livelihoods and on economic development in long-run. A comprehensive study by Blanton et al. (2019) has however assessed the impact of financial crises (currency crises, banking crises, inflation crises and debt crises) on women's wellbeing across 68 countries from 1980 to 2010 with different time lags since the end of a crisis. The findings consistently show the struggles women face in participating in the formal economy and in the public sphere, while also experiencing declines in health outcomes and educational achievement, up to seven years after a crisis ends.

From a relational lens on gender, economic recovery would precisely place care and gender equality at its heart. In line with Karamessini and Rubery (2013), Bargawi and Cozzi (2017) are in favour of engendering the economic recovery from a financial crisis which go through investment in "feminine" types of sectors such as health, care and education services, rather than traditional investments in "masculine" types of sectors such as constructions and physical infrastructure.

Gender-sensitive budgets at the macro-level, and fiscal policies supporting "feminine" types of sectors can improve women's visibility in the economy, as long as such effort is not undermined by austerity measures which tend to transmit the burden of budget cuts on the informal and household economy. Neo-classical austerity measures as such totally misunderstands the relational aspects of market and non-market outcomes, which goes back the essence of its starting assumption on self-interest where the "self" is atomistic and gender neutral. Hence, a gendered approach that alleviates the negative impact of financial crises on women needs to carefully consider the intertwined effects of the financial, productive and reproductive spheres of the economy (Elson, 2010). In effect, investments in the financial or productive spheres without support in the reproductive sphere might indeed have counterproductive effects in terms of aggregate welfare, cancelling out the initial support given. Instead of classical duality of gender, one must look at the synergies between genders and across the three spheres for the economy to be resilient in the event of a crisis, but also for preventing financial crises in the first place. For example, in the context of the climate and health crises of the 2020s, the duality of gender vanishes if one applies the perceived feminine attribute of "care" to the traditional "masculine" sectors of construction or finance. In effect, the essential criterion in decision-making for the construction sector should be the long-term impact on environmental and human health. As such governments should be making "mission-oriented" investments with private-public partnerships for a Green New Deal (Mazzucato, 2021). Similarly, in the financial sector, reaping the long-term benefits for environmental and human health should be the key criterion for successful green bonds provided by investment banks, rather than allowing speculative bubbles to be freely built up by herd-behaviour and social status-seeking in financial markets, with its devastating effects on the long-run sustainability of the economy.

Box 2.1 Methodological Warning: Group-Based Data and Data Availability

The empirical analyses in this Chapter make use of individual-level data aggregated at the group level. As such, it allows to focus on the explanatory power of group membership in the dynamics of accumulation of capital and labour earnings. Hence, Augmented Dickey Fuller (ADF) tests are conducted on time-series group earnings to be able find potential differences between groups on the nature of their earning variables (Tables 2.1 and 2.2), and Vector Auto-Regressions (VARs) of paired earnings between two demographic groups at a time are also performed to analyse the relationships between group earnings (Tables 2.3 and 2.4). The lack of availability of long-run time-series on demographic earnings by identity group across countries means that not enough data points were available to run a cointegration analysis, as done previously in Arestis et al. (2014). This calls for a more systematic collection of socio-demographic characteristics for income and wealth data over time, at the household, national and international level.

2.3 Labour Earnings by Race, Ethnicity, Gender and Occupation

2.3.1 *The US Experience (1968–2011)*

Using the Current Population Survey (CPS) data (King et al., 2010), this first case study looks at the long-run behaviour of earnings by gender and racial groups across occupations in the US labour force between 1968 and 2011. In accordance with the literature on the US stratification using CPS data (Arestis et al., 2014), the gender and racial identity group included are white men (wm), black men (bm), Hispanic men (hm), white women (wf), black women (bf), and Hispanic women (hf). We use the current annual weekly earnings of the above mentioned identity groups for 27 consistent occupational groups over the period 1968–2011, as displayed in Table 2.1, respectively. Earnings are the annual average of usual weekly earnings of employed full-time wage and salary workers by group.

Using Augmented Dickey-Fuller (ADF) tests, the methodology consists of testing whether the earnings of each identity group in each occupation are non-stationary, trend-stationary or stationary over the analysed period. By doing so, we are able to categorise the pattern followed by the earnings of each group across occupations according to the nature of the long-run trend. We use nominal instead of real earnings to account for money illusion including price stickiness, and lack of inflation-indexation on labour contracts and laws. We use means rather than median earnings in order to account for the information provided by outliers. In other words, we are interested in exploring the raw information provided by groups' earnings along the income stratification spectrum. If the earnings variable of an identity group is non-stationary, it means that there is a persistent cumulation of past effects (shocks) (Hendry & Juselius, 2001) leading to sustained changes in earnings. If the earnings variable of an identity group is stationary, it means that their earnings remain constant over the period. Stationary earnings are not benefiting from the increase in occupational earnings over the period and they are assumed to be compensating for a movement of income towards non-stationary earnings. Hence, non-stationary (stochastic trend) earnings are "elitist" in comparison to trend-stationary (deterministic-trend) or stationary earnings in the sense that a percentile of income distribution experiences shocks that cumulate in the long-run while other percentiles do not. In effect, trend-stationary "non-elitist" earnings represent a percentile of income distribution whose long-run trend grow at an arithmetic rate, while stationary "non-elitist" earnings represent a percentile of income distribution whose long-run trend is constant.

Looking at Table 2.1, apart from health and personal services with 89 and 78% female labour force, it shows that white men experience non-stationary earnings across all occupations. In comparison, black and Hispanic men experience trend-stationary and/or stationary earnings in many occupations, in professional occupations in particular. Black men experience stationary and trend-stationary earnings in a wider variety of occupations than Hispanic men. For example, in managerial occupations, the earnings of Hispanic men are non-stationary while the earnings of

Table 2.1 Augmented Dickey Fuller (ADF) tests on group labour earnings by US occupation in the period 1968–2011

	Non-stationary earnings	Trend-stationary earnings	Stationary earnings	Female labour share in 2011(%)
Exec., Adm. and Man. occupations				
1. Managerial occupations	wm_t hm_t wf_t bf_t hf_t	bm_t		41.3
2. Management related occupations	wm_t bm_t hm_t wf_t bf_t	hf_t		55.5
Professional occupations				
3. Engineers and Scientists	wm_t wf_t	bm_t hm_t bf_t	bm_μ hm_μ hf_μ	23.7
4. Health diagnosing occ.	wm_t wf_t bf_t	bm_t hm_t	bm_μ	77
5. Teachers	wm_t wf_t bf_t	bm_t hm_t	bm_μ hm_μ hf_μ	74.5
6. Social Scientists and Urban Planners	wm_t wf_t	bm_t hm_t bf_t	bm_μ hm_μ bf_μ hf_μ	53.2
7. Social, Recreations, and Religious Workers	wm_t wf_t	hm_t bf_t	hm_μ bf_μ hf_μ	63.8
8. Lawyers and Judges	wm_t wf_t	bm_t hm_t bf_t	bm_μ	36.2
9. Writers, Artists, Entertainers, and Athletes	wm_t wf_t	bm_t hm_t bf_t	bm_μ hm_μ bf_μ hf_μ	47
10. Technicians	wm_t bm_t hm_t wf_t bf_t			51.2
11. Sales occupations	wm_t hm_t wf_t bf_t		bm_μ	51.3
12. Administrative support occ.	wm_t hm_t wf_t bf_t	bm_t bf_t		73.8
Service occupations				
13. Household services	wm_t hm_t wf_t bf_t	bm_t	bm_μ	90
14. Protective services	wm_t bm_t hm_t	wf_t bf_t		21.2
15. Food services	wm_t bm_t hm_t wf_t bf_t			56.4
16. Health services	wf_t bf_t	wm_t bm_t hm_t	wm_μ bm_μ hm_μ hf_μ	88.8
17. Cleaning and Building	wm_t bm_t hm_t wf_t	bf_t	bf_μ	32.4
18. Personal services	bm_t wf_t bf_t	wm_t hm_t	wm_μ hm_μ	78.5
19.Farming, forestry, fishing	wm_t bm_t hm_t wf_t bf_t			17.6
Precision production, craft, and repairs occ.				

(continued)

Table 2.1 (continued)

	Non-stationary earnings	Trend-stationary earnings	Stationary earnings	Female labour share in 2011(%)
20. Mechanics	wm_t bm_t hm_t wf_t	bf_t	bf_μ hf_μ	3.8
21. Construction trades	wm_t bm_t hm_t wf_t	bf_t	bf_μ hf_μ	2.2
22. Extractive occupations	wm_t bm_t	hm_t wf_t	wf_μ	0.5
23. Precision occupations	wm_t bm_t hm_t	wf_t bf_t	hf_μ	32.7
Operators, fabricators, and labourers				
24. Operators	wm_t bm_t hm_t wf_t	bf_t		33
25. Transportation occupations	wm_t bm_t hm_t	wf_t bf_t		11.8
26. Material moving occupations	wm_t bm_t hm_t wf_t		bf_μ hf_μ	15.2
27. Military occupations	wm_t bm_t hm_t wf_t	bf_t	bf_μ hf_μ	9.7

Source: Charles and Vujic (2018)

Note: Only significant ADF results (5% or 10% level) with a trend t or constant μ are displayed for earnings of white men (wm), black men (bm), Hispanic men (hm), white women (wf), black women (bf), Hispanic women (hf)

black men are stationary. Looking at the female part of the labour force, a similar racial and ethnic dichotomy whereby white women experience non-stationary earnings across most occupations, while black and Hispanic women experience non-stationary earnings in only a few occupations. Here, trend-stationary and stationary earnings for the black and Hispanic groups go beyond professional occupations and affect most part of the labour force.

Overall, answering the question whether earnings can be conceptualised at the group rather than individual level in the US labour force is dominated by the fact that earnings of white workers display cumulative past effects (shocks) across most occupations and gender groups sustaining the social perception of an elitist group over other demographic groups.

2.3.2 *The UK Experience (2001–2014)*

Using the Labour Force Survey (LFS) data, this second case study looks at the long-run behaviour of earnings by gender and racial groups across occupations in the UK labour force in the period between 2001 and 2014. The gender and racial identity group included are white women (wf), non-white women (nwf), white men (wm),

Table 2.2 Augmented Dickey Fuller (ADF) tests on group labour earnings by UK occupation in the period 2001Q2–2014Q3

	Non-stationary earnings	Trend-stationary earnings	Stationary earnings	Female labour share across all years and quarters (%)
1. Managers and senior officials		wm, nwm, wf, nwf		34.85
2. Professional occupations	wf	wm, nwm, nwf		46.38
3. Associate professional and technical occupations		wm, nwm, wf, nwf		49.45
4. Administrative and secretarial occupations	wm (net), nwm (gross), wf	wm (gross), nwm (net), nwf		80.46
5. Skilled trades occupations		wm, nwm, wf, nwf		8.82
6. Personal service occupations	wm, wf	nwf, nwm		84.60
7. Sales and customer service occupations	wf (net), nwf (gross)	wm, nwm, wf (gross), nwf (net)		69.48
8. Process, Plant and machine operatives	wm	nwm, wf, nwf		14.16
9. Elementary occupations	wm, wf (gross)	nwm, wf (net), nwf		47.62

Source: Charles and Vujic (2018)
Note: Only significant ADF results (5% or 10% level) with a trend t or constant μ are displayed for earnings (gross and net) of white men (wm), non-white men (nwm), white women (wf), and non-white women (nwf)

and non-white men (nwm). We use the weekly gross (net) pay in the main job and the data is aggregated from the individual level as means per quarter. The nine occupational groups using SOC 2000 codes "occupation" are consistent over the period 2001Q2-2014Q4. Using the same methodology than for the US case study above, the results for each identity group *wf*, *nwf*, *wm*, and *nwm* are displayed in Table 2.2.

Starting with the comparison between white and non-white women in Table 2.2, the white female group experiences non-stationary earnings in four out of the nine types of occupations. In comparison, the non-white female group experiences trend-stationary earnings in all occupations. Similarly for the male groups, the white male group experiences non-stationary earnings in four out of the nine types of occupations. In comparison, the non-white male group experiences trend-stationary earnings in all occupations. Overall, answering the question whether earnings are elitist at the group level in the UK labour force is dominated by the fact that earnings of the white labour force display cumulative past effects (shocks) across many occupations and gender groups.

Table 2.3 Significant relationships of labour and capital earnings between demographic groups in the United Kingdom (1969–2016)

	Labour earnings at time *t*						Capital earnings at time *t*					
	Male	Female	White	Mixed	Asian	Black	Male	Female	White	Mixed	Asian	Black
Managerial and professional occupations												
Male (t-1)	+	+					+	+				
Female (t-1)	.	.					.	+				
White (t-1)			- ++	.	.	+			- . .	+	.	.
Mixed (t-1)			+	.					.	–		
Asian (t-1)			.		+				.		.	.
Black (t-1)			.			.			.			
Other skilled occupations												
Male (t-1)	+	+					–	–				
Female (t-1)	.	.					+	+				
White (t-1)			+++	+	.	+			- . .	–	.	.
Mixed (t-1)			–	.					.	+		
Asian (t-1)			.		.				.		.	
Black (t-1)			.			.			.			.
Elementary occupations												
Male (t-1)	+	+					.	.				
Female (t-1)	–	.					.	.				
White (t-1)			+++	+	.	+			+.+	+	.	.
Mixed (t-1)			.	–					.	.		
Asian (t-1)			.		.				+		.	
Black (t-1)			.			.			+			+

Source: Charles and Sguotti (2021)

Note: Signs representing the significant coefficients in the VARs of capital and labour earnings by occupation, gender, and ethnicity in the United Kingdom (12 Waves 1969–2016)—the dots representing the non-significant coefficients

Table 2.4 Significant relationships of labour and capital earnings between demographic groups in France (1978–2010)

	Labour earnings at time *t*								Capital earnings at time *t*							
	Male	Female	French	French Naturalized	Non-citizen	African citizenship	North-African	European	Male	Female	French	French Naturalized	Non-citizen	African citizenship	North-African	European
Managerial and professional occupations																
Male (t-1)	.	.							.	.						
Female (t-1)	+	+							+	+						
French (t-1)			+++++	+	−	+	+	+			− + − +	−		−	+	+
Nat.F (t-1)			−	−							+	−				
Non-cit (t-1)			−		−											
African (t-1)			+			−					+			−		
N-Afr (t-1)			.				.				−				+	
Europ. (t-1)			.					.			−					.
Other skilled occupations																
Male (t-1)	.	+							−	.						
Female (t-1)	.	.							+	+						
French (t-1)			- ++++	−	+	.	.	.			- - ++	+		−	.	+
Nat.F (t-1)			+	+							−	+				
Non-cit (t-1)			+		−											
African (t-1)			.			.					+			−		
N-Afr (t-1)			.				.				.				.	
Europ. (t-1)			.					.			.					−
Elementary occupations																
Male (t-1)	.	.							.	.						
Female (t-1)	.	.							+	+						
French (t-1)			++. + .	+	+	.	.	.			− + −	.		−	+	.
Nat.F (t-1)			+	.							+	+				
Non-cit (t-1)			.		.											

(continued)

Table 2.4 (continued)

African (t-1)			.			.					+			−		
N-Afr (t-1)			.				.				−				+	
Europ. (t-1)			.					.								.

Source: Charles and Sguotti (2021)

Note: Signs representing the significant coefficients in the VARs of capital and labour earnings by occupation, gender, and ethnicity in the United Kingdom (12 Waves 1969–2016)—the dots representing the non-significant coefficients

2.4 Group "Legitimacy" in Financial Flows[3]

Starting from Charles and Vujic (2018), we assumed a society with two demographic groups, *i* and *j*, both belonging to the same occupational group k. Therefore, individuals are composed of groups *i* and *k* or of group identities *j* and *k*. A socially dominant group is represented by *j* and receives a premium for group membership, while the non-dominant group is represented by *i*, whose earnings are discriminated against due to group membership. Hence, we assumed a ranking of groups of $j > i$, dependent upon the context specificity in which this ranking has been socially and historically determined.

Box 2.2 Methodological Warning: Causality Vs. Correlation

In mainstream economics textbooks, we learn that individual income is a function of a variety of human capital factors, such as marginal productivity, educational background, skills, and so on. Such methodological individualism means that the discriminatory elements of socialization attached to gender, race, class, ethnicity and other social identities are embedded across those individual characteristics and are, as such, not fully accounted for to explain the variance in individuals' income. As a result, when seeking causal links to explain the variance in income using first-differences, the historical elements of discrimination accumulated over time may end up in the residual of a traditional regression. However, such discriminatory elements describing the power relationships between social groups in a particular context become central to the way income is distributed and hence the way wealth is accumulated over time. "Correlation is not causality" we have been taught, and that's right. However, correlation tells us a story of relationality between variables whose inherent nature lie in the long-term relationship that have generated engrained long-term links difficult to depart from—similarly to the cognitive biases deeply engrained in remembered utility. We have been taught to "de-naturalize" time series data by de-trending, differentiating and searching for immutable causal links. However, when context shapes economic outcomes, the causals links A ➔ B and B ➔ C in one context might become B ➔ A and C ➔ B in another. Hence, the methodology of the time-series analysis in this chapter (1) uses level data to keep the nature of the time series alive, including potential structural breaks, and then applies (2) Augmented Dickey Fuller (ADF) tests on group earnings to analyse the nature of the long-run trends, and (3) Vector Autoregression (VAR) to analyse the nature of the relationships between group earnings. As such, we can highlight the context and nature of the relations present in the time series analysed.

[3] This section draws from Charles and Sguotti (2021).

At the societal level, the sum of earnings from capital and labour $z = \sum (r + w)$ is then distributed between all groups, such that $Z = \sum_{k=0}^{n} (z_i + z_j)$. The point of the model is to show the nature of the short-run relationships of labour and capital earnings between *i* and *j*, whether the relationship is statistically significant (positively or negatively), or non-significant. In other words, the model describes the share of the capital and labour earnings going towards *i* and *j* in Z. In the short run, at one end of the individualist spectrum, the first scenario is that capital earnings per group *i* and *j* at the occupational level *k* will depend on the group's productivity and on its earnings in the previous period, calculated as follows:

$$\begin{cases} r_{j(t)} = \alpha + \beta_1 r_{j(t-1)} + \varepsilon_t \\ r_{i(t)} = \alpha + \beta_3 r_{i(t-1)} + \varepsilon_t \end{cases} \tag{2.1}$$

where capital earnings per demographic group at time *t* depends on a constant, on its previous value at time *t* – 1, and a white noise term, while labour earnings will be calculated as follows:

$$\begin{cases} w_{j(t)} = \alpha + \beta_1 w_{j(t-1)} + \varepsilon_t \\ w_{i(t)} = \alpha + \beta_3 w_{i(t-1)} + \varepsilon_t \end{cases} \tag{2.2}$$

where labour earnings per demographic group at time *t* depends on a constant, on its previous value at time *t* – 1, and a white noise term. Equations (2.1) and (2.2) work simultaneously in Z.

To test whether past earning trends have experienced elements of group behaviour with a premium attached to group *j*, the following Vector Autoregression analysis is conducted with the following earning relationships:

$$\begin{cases} r_{j(t)} = \alpha + \beta_1 r_{j(t-1)} + \beta_2 r_{i(t-1)} + \varepsilon_t \\ r_{i(t)} = \alpha + \beta_3 r_{i(t-1)} + \beta_4 r_{j(t-1)} + \varepsilon_t \end{cases} \tag{2.3}$$

where capital earnings per demographic group at time *t* depends on a constant, on its previous value at time *t* – 1, on the value of the other group's earnings at time *t* – 1, and a white noise term; while labour earnings will be:

$$\begin{cases} w_{j(t)} = \alpha + \beta_1 w_{j(t-1)} + \beta_2 w_{i(t-1)} + \varepsilon_t \\ w_{i(t)} = \alpha + \beta_3 w_{i(t-1)} + \beta_4 w_{j(t-1)} + \varepsilon_t \end{cases} \tag{2.4}$$

where labour earnings per demographic group at time *t* depends on a constant, on its previous value at time *t* – 1, on the value of the other group's earnings at time *t* – 1, and a white noise term.

At the other end of the spectrum, a second scenario is that, if group membership influences the dynamics of earnings between groups, then Eqs. (2.3) and (2.4) in Z will apply. Here, the nature of the earning relationships between i and j will depend on the sign and statistical significance of β_1 and β_2 for (2.3), and β_3 and β_4 for (2.4). From this perspective, group membership is socially assigned by a dominant convention rather than chosen individually, consciously, or unconsciously, and reproduced over time. While the constant α represents the labour earning gaps between i and j in (2.4) and the capital earning gaps between i and j in (2.3), the analysis is more concerned with the short-run dynamics of group biases. The results in Tables 2.3 and 2.4 presented in the next section are therefore concerned with the sign and statistical significance of β_1 and β_2 for (2.3), and β_3 and β_4 for (2.4), while the α gaps are displayed in the Appendix. Furthermore, as described above, context matters for the ways by which income is generated and wealth is accumulated by a social group over time. Therefore, groups i and j and occupation k will differ across countries. Hence, the empirical testing of Eqs. (2.1)–(2.4) was applied to the United Kingdom and France depending on country-dependent classifications.

In terms of methodology, for the United Kingdom and France, individual data on labour and capital earnings were aggregated at the group level, including gender, class, immigrant status, and other demographic variables depending on the country's classifications (LIS, 2020). LIS (2020) is a harmonized database of microdata on income and other economic personal and household variables. Labour and capital earning variables were plotted for each country and group, below, to test Eqs. (2.1) to (2.4) for each country. VARs allowed us to generalize the dependencies of two variables over time, as displayed in Eqs. (2.3) and (2.4), using LIS data (2020, Kirchgässner et al., 2013). Tables 2.3 and 2.4 are simple visual representations of the VARs shown in the Appendix, as they display only the signs of the statistically significant coefficients β_1 to β_4 in Eqs. (2.1) to (2.4) of the model described above—the dots representing the non-significant coefficients. The limitation of the data-driven methodology is essential in terms of the various combinations of relationships that can be inferred. Hence, prior knowledge of the historical relationships between demographic groups, together with the availability of data representing these groups, is crucial for the validity of the model.

2.4.1 Capital and Labour Earnings in the UK (1994–2016)

In the United Kingdom, the breakdown of the capital and labour earnings based on LIS data (2020) are by gender and ethnicity (white, mixed race, Asian, and Black), with three main occupations (managers and professionals, other skilled workers, and labourers/elementary), as displayed in Table 2.5 of the Appendix. Figure 2.1 represents the average labour income for the white and Black groups from 1994 to 2016. While the Black trend starts to overtake the white trend in the mid-2000s, the Great Recession brought the trends back to their "normal" dominant–dominated relationship.

Figure 2.2 shows the average of all cash payments from property and capital (including financial and non-financial assets—interest and dividends, rental income,

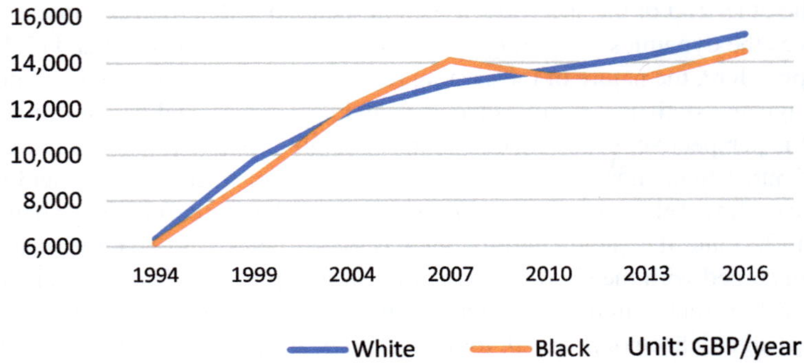

Fig. 2.1 Average labour income by ethnicity in the United Kingdom (1994–2016). Source: Charles and Sguotti (2021)

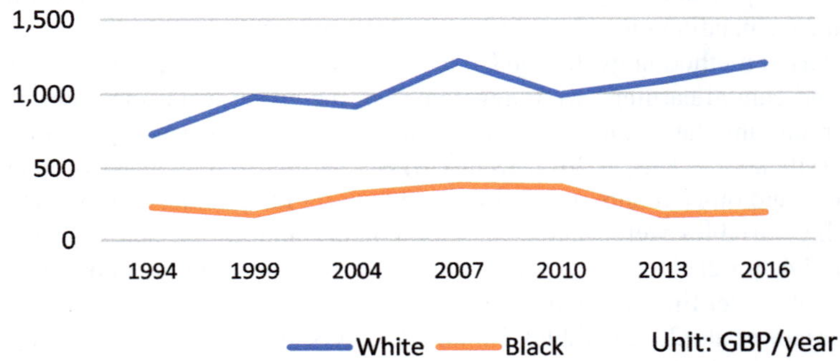

Fig. 2.2 Average capital income by ethnicity in the United Kingdom (1994–2016). Source: Charles and Sguotti (2021)

and royalties) for the Black and white groups. The evolution of the existing gap is quite significant in describing the relationship of power between the two groups in financial accumulation. While the white group benefited from a sharp increase in capital income in the build-up towards the Great Recession, the trend for the Black group was stagnant in the same period, followed by an increasing capital income gap. Here, again, the interdependence of group earnings over time is striking.

Looking at the VARs in Table 2.5 of the Appendix, numerous coefficients β1 to β4 across occupations are statistically significant at the 5 or 10% level. This points towards an interdependency of capital and labour earnings between groups at the occupational level, which is more visible in Table 2.3, below, reporting the signs of the statistically significant coefficients from the VARs of Table 2.5.

The relationships of labour and capital earnings displayed in Table 2.3 would reflect Eqs. (2.1) and (2.2) if all signs in the grey diagonals were positive and none of the other cases were positive or negative. Instead, we see a pattern emerging here whereby, on the one hand, the male and white group's labour earnings at time $t-1$ are positively correlated with female labour earnings at time t, and with the labour earnings of the mixed and Black groups across all three occupations. On the other hand, labour earnings at t − 1 of the minority groups tend not to be significant with their own earnings at time t. For capital earnings, statistical significance is not as widespread, given the extent of the wealth gaps between the dominant and minority groups. It is worth noting, however, that there is a strong interdependence of earnings in the elementary occupations with the capital earnings of minority groups at time t − 1 being positively related to the capital earnings of the white group at time t.

2.4.2 *Capital and Labour Earnings in France (1978–2010)*

In France, the breakdown of the capital and labour earnings based on LIS data (2020) are by gender and citizenship (French, French-naturalized, non-citizen, African, Northern African, European, and others), with three main occupations (managers and professionals, other skilled workers, and labourers/elementary), as displayed in Table 2.6 of the Appendix.

Figures 2.3 and 2.4 represent the trends of labour and capital income by class from 1978 to 2010 in France. The trends of labour income show an increasing gap since the 1990s between white-collar and blue-collar workers, while skilled workers experienced trend-stationary labour income over the period. For the trends of capital income, there is a similar increasing gap between white-collar workers and the other two groups, and all three trends were hit by the Great Recession of 2008. Overall, such data shows that, regardless of skills, productivity, or ethnic background, the rising gap shows that there is a pattern of a dominating–dominated relationship, horizontally, between white-collar workers and the other two categories.

Looking at the VARs in Table 2.6 of the Appendix, numerous coefficients β1 to β4 across occupations are statistically significant at the 5 or 10% level. This points towards an interdependency of capital and labour earnings between groups at the occupational level, which is more visible in Table 2.4, below, reporting the signs of the statistically significant coefficients from the VARs of Table 2.6.

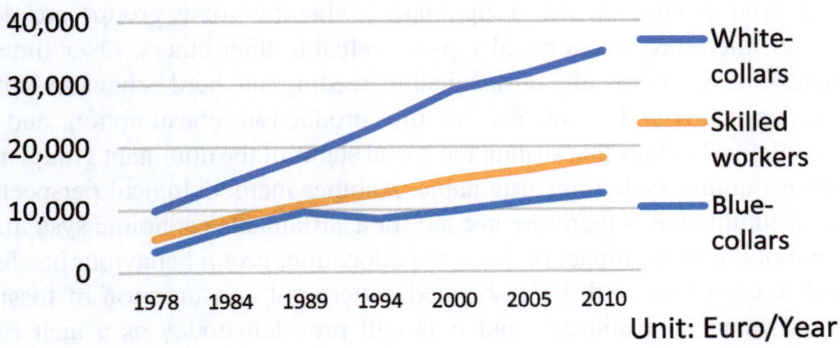

Fig. 2.3 Average labour income by class in France (1978–2010). Source: Charles and Sguotti (2021)

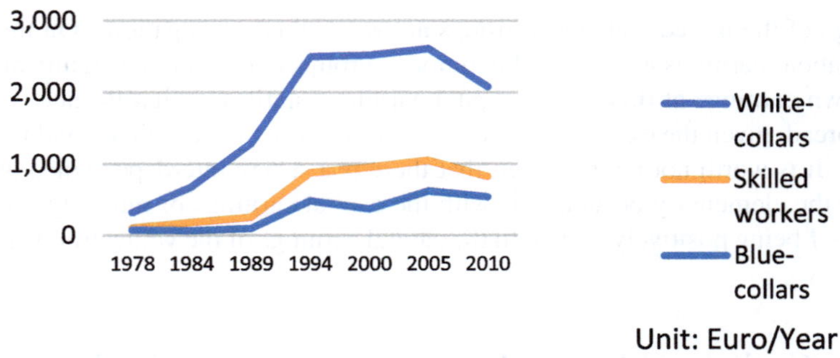

Fig. 2.4 Average capital income by class in France (1978–2010). Source: Charles and Sguotti (2021)

The relationships of labour and capital earnings displayed in Table 2.4 would again reflect Eqs. (2.1) and (2.2) if all signs in the grey diagonals were positive and none of the other cases were positive or negative. Instead, there is a similar pattern of interdependence between the dominant French group and minority groups for labour earnings, whereby the labour earnings of French nationals are correlated significantly to the earnings of minority groups, especially in managerial and professional occupations. Meanwhile, the gender element of group behaviour shows in the labour earnings of men in managerial and professional occupations, and in the capital earnings across occupations, whereby the earnings of women at time $t - 1$ are positively correlated to male earnings at time t.

Overall, the results across the three countries show that for some occupations, there is a strong interdependence of earnings, pointing toward Models (3) and (4), and the results reflecting more in Models (1) and (2) tend to be for male earnings, for the dominant incumbent group (white or nationals), and for labour earnings rather than capital earnings. Some social groups earn more at the expense of others, which is based on social relationships of power more than on individual productivity. There is, therefore, the evidence here of the interdependency of earnings between social groups, whether it is in the United Kingdom, France, or Italy, with varying degrees of interdependency across groups and countries. Such discrepancies are not based on individual productivity but on group biases, whereby some groups are deemed socially and, therefore, economically more valuable than others. Over time, such discrepancies are economically unsustainable, feeding into herd behaviour that exacerbates group status and eventually creating production, consumption, and financially speculative bubbles that sustain the social status of the dominant group, making the entire economic system unsustainable. Another methodological perspective on financial accumulation is therefore needed for a sustainable economic system.

When looking at its impact on resource allocation, group behaviour has fed into the Great Acceleration with its associated patterns of consumption of fossil fuel, natural and financial resources, and it is still prevalent today as a tacit rule for resource allocation. The pattern of earnings accumulation in Western economies is still dependent upon colonial and patriarchal dominance of certain dominant groups at the expense of dominated groups. In that respect, Tables 2.4 and 2.5 have illustrated how group membership influences positively or negatively income accumulation between demographic groups in the U.K and France over the past decades. The overall finding from both Tables is that there is no significant relationships between the past and present earnings of minority groups, while most significant relationships exist for the dominant groups, White and Male in the UK sample, and the French nationality group in the France sample. For example, in Table 2.5, it doesn't make "economic" sense to have the past earnings of non-French groups being positively associated with the present earnings of the French nationality group. Similarly, looking at capital earnings across occupations, it doesn't make economic sense for male capital earnings at time *t* to be positively associated with female capital earnings at time *t-1*, and it provides yet more evidence for a system of financial accumulation based on group rather than individual behaviour.

2.5 Towards Sustainable Earnings?

While the global patterns of wealth accumulation have been well-documented by Piketty (2014, 2019), and that income inequality tends to be broken down by income strata (Milanovic, 2016), or sectoral level (Galbraith, 2012), dividing earnings between labour and capital is a methodological choice which allows to investigate the dynamics of income accumulation in both the labour and capital shares of national income. Segregating further by demographic group is a theoretical choice which, depending on data availability by country, highlights the patterns of income accumulation affected by group membership. Group memberships are in effect setting the tacit rules of income distribution at the margin and hence over time.

In such a dynamic system of social relationships, analysing financial flows takes us back to the classical literature on the nature of money with trust being at to the heart of the meaning of money from Aristotle to Keynes (Eich, 2022). In a dynamic system of financial flows based of social relationships, trust is shaped by those tacit rules. Over the past forty years, the pattern of financial accumulation based of those tacit rules have led to a mistrust and misfunctioning of the economic system to self-regulate income accumulation. The financialisation process fed by a process of "financing finance" (Mazzucato, 2021) is now leading to a two-tier system going in the hands of a few dominant groups at the top of the income distribution, while leaving labour earners with stagnant real-wages at the bottom. This Chapter also shows that dominated groups have experienced a colonisation of their labour earnings based of vicious marginal increases for some groups at the expense of other groups. Meanwhile, mapping the social identity elements of those few would lead to a biased sample of the global human population, but such demographic data is not available.

So, are the current patterns of group accumulation sustainable? Well, if sustainability is understood as a self-sustaining process of earning accumulation, then the current tacit rules on group norms are certainly self-sustainable and here to stay. However, if sustainability is understood as the extent to which current earnings feed into a resilient economic system able to feed the financial needs of sustaining life on Earth, then no.

Appendix

Table 2.5 VARs of capital and labour earnings by occupation, gender, and ethnicity in the United Kingdom (12 Waves 1969–2016)

Variables Names	Oc1: Managers and Professionals (ISCO 1 & 2) Oc2: Other Skilled Workers (ISCO 3–8, 10) Oc3: Labourers/Elementary (ISCO 9) lab: Average Labour Income cap: Average Capital Income m: Male Population f: Female Population eth1: White Ethnic Group eth2: Mixed Race/Multiple Ethnic Groups eth3: ASIAN/ASIAN BRITISH ETHNIC GROUP eth4: BLACK/AFRICAN/CARIBBEAN/BLACK BRITISH ETHNIC GROUP ** Significance ≤0.05 * Significance between 0.10 and 0.05
Variables	*VARs*
oc1_mlab oc1_flab	Oc1_mlab = 6802.64 * + 0.91 oc1_mlab ($t-1$) – 0.01 oc1_flab ($t-1$) Oc1_flab = 2763.66 ** + 0.75 oc1_mlab ($t-1$) – 0.12 oc1_flab ($t-1$)
oc1_mcap oc1_fcap	Oc1_mcap = 836.92 * + 1.36 oc1_mcap ($t-1$)—1.01 oc1_fcap ($t-1$) Oc1_fcap = 762.79 * +0.70 oc1_mcap ($t-1$) – 0.40 oc1_oc1_fcap ($t-1$)
oc1_eth1lab oc1_eth2lab	Oc1_eth1lab = 60071.24 * – 0.77 * oc1_eth1lab ($t-1$) + 0.25 * oc1_eth2lab ($t-1$) Oc1_eth2lab = 45526.60–0.52 oc1_eth1lab ($t-1$) + 0.36 oc1_eth2lab ($t-1$)
oc1_eth1cap oc1_eth2cap,	Oc1_eth1cap = 2930.56 * – 0.60* oc1_eth1cap ($t-1$) – 0.17 oc1_eth2cap ($t-1$) Oc1_eth2cap = –691.47 * + 0.85* oc1_eth1 cap ($t-1$) – 0.01 oc1_eth2cap ($t-1$)
oc1_eth1lab oc1_eth3lab	Oc1_eth1lab = 18249.62 * + 0.53 * oc1_eth1lab ($t-1$) + 0.04 oc1_eth3lab ($t-1$) Oc1_eth3lab = –12984.76 + 0.79 oc1_eth1lab ($t-1$) + 0.55 ** oc1_eth3lab ($t-1$)
oc1_eth1cap oc1_eth3cap,	Oc1_eth1cap = 1758.42 * – 0.10 oc1_eth1cap ($t-1$) + 0.16 oc1_eth3cap ($t-1$) Oc1_eth3cap = 494.53–0.37 oc1_eth1cap ($t-1$) + 1.44 oc1_eth3cap ($t-1$)
oc1_eth1lab oc1_eth4lab	Oc1_eth1lab = 18040.16 * + 0.54 * oc1_eth1lab ($t-1$) +0.02 oc1_eth4lab ($t-1$) Oc4_eth4lab = – 21267.1 + 1.71 * oc1_eth1lab ($t-1$) – 0.24 oc1_eth4lab ($t-1$)
oc1_eth1cap oc1_eth4cap	Oc1_eth1cap = 1749.47 * – 0.02 oc1_eth1cap ($t-1$) – 0.04 oc1_eth4cap ($t-1$) Oc1_eth4cap = –621.16 + 0.67 oc1_eth1cap ($t-1$) + 0.01 oc1_eth4cap ($t-1$)
oc2_mlab oc2_flab	Oc2_mlab = 3155.20 * + 1.25 * oc2_mlab ($t-1$) – 0.49 oc2_flab ($t-1$) Oc2_flab = 1113.26 * + 0.72 * oc2_mlab ($t-1$) – 0.11 oc2_flab ($t-1$)

(continued)

Table 2.5 (continued)

oc2_mcap oc2_fcap	Oc2_mcap = 223.20 * − 4.11 * oc2_mcap (*t* − 1) + 4.29 * oc2_fcap (*t* − 1) Oc2_fcap = 241.35 * 2212 3.47 * oc2_mcap (*t* − 1) + 3.83 * oc2_fcap (*t* − 1)
oc2_eth1lab oc2_eth2lab,	Oc2_eth1lab = −3702.57 * +1.50 * oc2_eth1lab (*t* − 1)—0.27 * oc2_eth2lab (*t* − 1) oc2_eth2lab = −18432.94 + 2.75 ** oc2_eth1lab (*t* − 1)—0.80 oc2_eth2lab (*t* − 1)
oc2_eth1cap oc2_eth2cap,	Oc2_eth1cap = 1160.31 * − 0.48 * oc2_eth1cap (*t* − 1)—0.01 oc2_eth2cap (*t* − 1) Oc2_eth2cap = 2745.67 * − 3.43 * oc2_eth1cap (*t* − 1) +0.50 * oc2_eth2cap (*t* − 1)
oc2_eth1lab oc2_eth3lab	Oc2_eth1lab = 7065.82 * + 0.68 * oc2_eth1lab (*t* − 1) + 0.01 oc2_eth3lab (*t* − 1) Oc2_eth3lab = −2555.72 + 0.77 oc2_eth1lab (*t* − 1) + 0.25 oc2_eth3lab (*t* − 1)
oc2_eth1cap oc2_eth3cap	Oc2_eth1cap = 362.58 + 0.32 oc2_eth1cap (*t* − 1) + 0.27 oc2_eth3cap (*t* − 1) Oc2_eth3cap = −209.81 + 0.76 oc2_eth1cap (*t* − 1) + 0.85 oc2_eth3cap (*t* − 1)
oc2_eth1lab oc2_eth4lab	Oc2_eth1lab = 6707.39 * + 0.76 * oc2_eth1lab (*t* − 1) − 0.05 oc2_eth4lab (*t* − 1) Oc2_eth4lab = 3224.54 + 0.84** oc2_eth1lab (*t* − 1) − 0.01 oc2_eth4lab (*t* − 1)
oc2_eth1cap oc2_eth4cap	Oc2_eth1cap = 617.83 * + 0.24 oc2_eth1cap (*t* − 1) − 0.25 oc2_eth4cap (*t* − 1) Oc2_eth4cap = 185.54 + 0.09 oc2_eth1cap (*t* − 1) − 0.45 oc2_eth4cap (*t* − 1)
oc3_mlab oc3_flab	Oc3_mlab = 1958.92 * + 1.30 * oc3_mlab (*t* − 1) − 0.73 ** oc3_flab (*t* − 1) Oc3_flab = 414.75 + 0.41* oc3_mlab (*t* − 1) + 0.22 oc3_flab (*t* − 1)
oc3_mcap oc3_fcap	Oc3_mcap = 261.07 * + 0.60 oc3_mcap (*t* − 1) − 0.47 oc3_fcap (*t* − 1) Oc3_fcap = 171.71 * + 0.36 oc3_mcap (*t* − 1)– 0.10 oc3_fcap (*t* − 1)
oc3_eth1lab oc3_eth2lab	Oc3_eth1lab = 6944.97 * + 0.47 * oc3_eth1lab (*t* − 1) − 0.02 oc3_eth2lab (*t* − 1) Oc3_eth2lab = −7280.15 + 2.17 * oc3_eth1lab (*t* − 1) − 0.71 * oc3_eth2lab (*t* − 1)
oc3_eth1cap oc3_eth2cap	Oc3_eth1cap = −333.46 * + 1.88 * oc3_eth1cap (*t* − 1) − 0.03 oc3_eth2cap (*t* − 1) Oc3_eth2cap = −742.18 * + 2.42 * oc3_eth1cap (t − 1) − 0.25 ** oc3_eth2cap (t − 1)
oc3_eth1lab oc3_eth3lab	Oc3_eth1lab = 4546.80 * + 0.64 * oc3_eth1lab (t − 1) + 0.03 oc3_eth3lab (t − 1) Oc3_eth3lab = −1565.27 + 1.24 oc3_eth1lab (t − 1) − 0.12 oc3_eth3lab (t − 1)
oc3_eth1cap oc3_eth3cap	Oc3_eth1cap = 80.42 + 0.53 oc3_eth1cap (t − 1) + 0.14 * oc3_eth3cap (t − 1) Oc3_eth3cap = 1657.60 ** − 4.40 oc3_eth1cap (t − 1) + 0.51 oc3_eth3cap (t − 1)

(continued)

oc3_eth1lab oc3_eth4lab	Oc3_eth1lab = 4729.1 * + 0.35 ** oc3_eth1lab (t − 1) + 0.27 oc3_eth4lab (t − 1) Oc3_eth4lab = 5102.60 * + 0.87 ** oc3_eth1lab (t − 1) − 0.19 oc3_eth4lab (t − 1)
oc3_eth1cap oc3_eth4cap	Oc3_eth1cap = −82.38 + 1.07 * oc3_eth1cap (*t* − 1) + 0.43 * oc3_eth4cap (*t* − 1) Oc3_eth4cap = 272.02–0.74 oc3_eth1cap (*t* − 1) + 0.56 ** oc3_eth4cap (*t* − 1)

Source: Charles and Sguotti (2021)

Table 2.6 VARs of capital and labour earnings by occupation, gender, and citizenship in France (7 Waves 1978–2010)

Variables Names	Oc1: Managers and Professionals (ISCO 1 & 2) Oc2: Other Skilled Workers (ISCO 3-8, 10) Oc3: Labourers/Elementary (ISCO 9) lab: Average Labour Income lap: Average Capital Income m: Male Population f: Female Population cit1: French Citizenship cit2: French Naturalized Citizens cit3: Non-Citizen Status cit4: African Citizenship Holder cit5: Norther African Citizenship Holder cit6 Europe Citizenship Holder ** Significance ≤0.05 * Significance between 0.10 and 0.05
Variables	*VARs*
oc1_mlab oc1_flab	Oc1_mlab = 10957.93 * − 0.23 oc1_mlab (*t* − 1) + 1.57 * oc1_flab (*t* − 1) Oc1_flab = 4123.91 * − 0.08 oc1_mlab (*t* − 1) + 1.12 * oc1_flab (*t* − 1)
oc1_mcap oc1_fcap	Oc1_mcap = 1058.91 * − 1.15 oc1_mcap (*t* − 1) + 1.92 * oc1_fcap (*t* − 1) Oc1_fcap = 949.85 * − 1.00 oc1_mcap (*t* − 1) + 1.68 ** oc1_fcap (*t* − 1)
oc1_cit1lab oc1_cit2lab	Oc1_cit1lab = −8355.29 * + 2.38 * oc1_cit1lab (*t* − 1) − 1.12 * oc1_cit2lab (*t* − 1) Oc1_cit2lab = −12208.73 * + 2.54 * oc1_cit1lab (*t* − 1) − 1.30 * oc1_cit2lab (*t* − 1)
oc1_cit1cap oc1_cit2cap	Oc1_cit1cap = 6732.47 * − 1.97 * oc1_cit1cap (*t* − 1) +0.49 * oc1_cit2cap (*t* − 1) Oc1_cit2cap = 12414.87 * − 2.78 * oc1_cit1cap (*t* − 1) − 1.85 * oc1_cit2cap (*t* − 1)
oc1_cit1lab oc1_cit3lab	Oc1_cit1lab = 7407.12 * +0.96 * oc1_cit1lab (*t* − 1) − 0.08 * oc1_cit3lab (*t* − 1) Oc1_cit3lab = 28943.92* − 0.05 * oc1_cit1lab (*t* − 1) − 0.43* oc1_cit3lab (*t* − 1)

(continued)

Table 2.6 (continued)

oc1_cit1cap oc1_cit3cap	Insufficient observations
oc1_cit1lab oc1_cit4lab	Oc1_cit1lab = 5027.05 * + 0.91 * oc1_cit1lab ($t-1$) + 0.11 * oc1_cit4lab ($t-1$) Oc1_cit4lab = −6861.91 + 0.95 * oc1_cit1lab ($t-1$) − 0.59 * oc1_cit4lab ($t-1$)
oc1_cit1cap oc1_cit4cap	Oc1_cit1cap = 1084.98 * + 0.42 * oc1_cit1cap($t-1$) + 0.76 * oc1_cit4cap($t-1$) Oc1_cit4cap = 1451.97 * − 0.30 * oc1_cit1cap ($t-1$) − 0.54 * oc1_cit4cap($t-1$)
oc1_cit1lab oc1_cit5lab	Oc1_cit1lab = 6963.37 * + 0.88 * oc1_cit1lab($t-1$) + 0.01 oc1_cit5lab($t-1$) Oc1_cit5lab = −825.88 + 0.59 * oc1_cit1lab($t-1$) − 0.13 oc1_cit5lab($t-1$)
oc1_cit1cap oc1_cit5cap	Oc1_cit1cap = 4648.04 * − 0.48 * oc1_cit1cap ($t-1$) − 7.97 * oc1_cit5cap($t-1$) Oc1_cit5cap = −2122.89 * + 7.96 * oc1_cit1cap($t-1$) +10.12 * oc1_cit5cap($t-1$)
oc1_cit1lab oc1_cit6lab	Oc1_cit1lab = 7543.65 * + 0.82 * oc1_cit1lab ($t-1$) + 0.07 oc1_cit6lab($t-1$) Oc1_cit6lab = −7046.77 + 1.10 * oc1_cit1lab ($t-1$) − 0.19 oc1_cit6lab($t-1$)
oc1_cit1cap oc1_cit6cap	Oc1_cit1cap =763.78 * +0.92 * oc1_cit1cap ($t-1$) − 0.41 * oc1_cit6cap($t-1$) Oc1_cit6cap = −284.33 + 0.90 * oc1_cit1cap($t-1$) − 0.24 oc1_cit6cap($t-1$)
oc2_mlab oc2_flab	Oc2_mlab = 4463.35 * + 0.41 oc2_mlab($t-1$) + 0.58 oc2_flab($t-1$) Oc2_flab = 2649.01 * + 0.55 ** oc2_mlab ($t-1$) +0.18 oc2_flab($t-1$)
oc2_mcap oc2_fcap,	Oc2_mcap = 233.10 * − 2.21 ** oc2_mcap ($t-1$) +2.60 * oc2_fcap($t-1$) Oc2_fcap = 301.11 * − 2.64 oc2_mcap ($t-1$) +3.02 ** oc2_fcap($t-1$)
oc2_cit1lab oc2_cit2lab	Oc2_cit1lab = −2299.50 * − 4.46 * oc2_cit1lab($t-1$) + 6.31 * oc2_cit2lab($t-1$) Oc2_cit2lab = 2662.28 * − 0.23 * oc2_cit1lab($t-1$) + 1.16 * oc2_cit2lab($t-1$)
oc2_cit1cap oc2_cit2cap	Oc2_cit1cap = 4507.12 * − 2.89 * oc2_cit1cap($t-1$) − 0.86 * oc2_cit2cap($t-1$) Oc2_cit2cap = 223.28 * + 0.22 * oc2_cit1cap($t-1$) + 0.24 * oc2_cit2cap($t-1$)
oc2_cit1lab oc2_cit3lab	Oc2_cit1lab = 5314.08 * + 0.65 * oc2_cit1ab ($t-1$) + 0.16 * oc2_cit3lab ($t-1$) Oc2_cit3lab = −1203.08 * + 1.47 * oc2_cit1lab($t-1$) − 0.69 * oc2_cit3lab($t-1$)
oc2_cit1cap oc2_cit3cap	Note: oc2_cit3cap dropped because of collinearity
oc2_cit1lab oc2_cit4lab	Oc2_cit1lab = 2513.95 + 0.96 * oc2_cit1lab($t-1$) − 0.03 oc2_cit4lab($t-1$) Oc2_cit4lab = 8809.76 + 0.17 oc2_cit1lab($t-1$) − 0.14 oc2_cit4lab($t-1$)

(continued)

Table 2.6 (continued)

oc2_cit1cap oc2_cit4cap	Oc2_cit1cap = 1509.01 * − 0.63 * oc2_cit1cap (t − 1) + 0.42 * oc2_cit4cap(t − 1) Oc2_cit4cap = 2000.28 * − 1.73 * oc2_cit1cap (t − 1) − 0.47 * oc2_cit4cap(t − 1)
oc2_cit1lab oc2_cit5lab	Oc2_cit1lab = 4838.81 * + 0.78 * oc2_cit1lab(t − 1) − 0.01 oc2_cit5lab(t − 1) Oc2_cit5lab = 5555.39 + 0.50 oc2_cit1lab(t − 1) − 0.20 oc2_cit5lab(t − 1)
oc2_cit1cap oc2_cit5cap	Oc2_cit1cap = 285.74 ** + 0.59 * oc2_cit1cap (t − 1) + 0.50 oc2_cit5cap(t − 1) Oc2_cit5cap = 118.19 + 0.20 oc2_cit1cap(t − 1) − 0.31 oc2_cit5cap(t − 1)
oc2_cit1lab oc2_cit6lab	Oc2_cit1lab = 4951.24 * + 0.71 * oc2_cit1lab(t − 1) + 0.07 oc2_cit6lab(t − 1) Oc2_cit6lab = 2088.77 + 0.79 oc2_cit1lab (t − 1) − 0.04 oc2_cit6lab(t − 1)
oc2_cit1cap oc2_cit6cap	Oc2_cit1cap = 292.98 ** + 1.08 ** oc2_cit1cap (t − 1) − 0.41 oc2_cit6cap(t − 1) Oc2_cit6cap =255.55 + 1.80 * oc2_cit1cap (t − 1) − 1.34 * oc2_cit6cap(t − 1)
oc3_mlab oc3_flab	Oc3_mlab = 6636.90 * − 0.50 oc3_mlab (t − 1) +1.20 oc3_flab(t − 1) Oc3_flab = 4424.80 * − 0.39 oc3_mlab(t − 1) + 1.06 oc3_flab (t − 1)
oc3_mcap oc3_fcap	Oc3_mcap = 169.64 ** − 2.54 oc3_mcap(t − 1) + 3.19 ** oc3_fcap (t − 1) Oc3_fcap = 172.83 * − 2.00 oc3_mcap(t − 1) +2.68 ** oc3_fcap(t − 1)
oc3_cit1lab oc3_cit2lab,	Oc3_cit1lab = −1601.95 * +0.08 * oc3_cit1lab(t − 1) + 1.20 * oc3_cit2lab(t − 1) Oc3_cit2lab = 1014.03 * + 0.09* oc3_cit1lab(t − 1) + 0.93 oc3_cit2lab(t − 1)
oc3_cit1cap oc3_cit2cap	Oc3_cit1cap = 940.38 * − 2.37 * oc3_cit1cap(t − 1) +2.55 * oc3_cit2cap (t − 1) Oc3_cit2cap = 896.50 * − 2.48 oc3_cit1cap(t − 1) + 2.22 * oc3_cit2cap(t − 1)
oc3_cit1lab oc3_cit3lab,	Oc3_cit1lab = 4745.62 * + 0.84 * oc3_cit1lab (t − 1) − 0.12 oc3_cit3lab(t − 1) Oc3_cit3lab = −300.11 * + 1.49 * oc3_cit1lab(t − 1) − 0.47 oc3_cit3lab(t − 1)
oc3_cit1cap oc3_cit3cap	Insufficient observations
oc3_cit1lab oc3_cit4lab	Oc3_cit1lab = 6848.13 + 0.30 oc3_cit1lab(t − 1) + 0.13 oc3_cit4lab(t − 1) Oc3_cit4lab = 9601.59–0.27 oc3_cit1lab(t − 1) + 0.11 oc3_cit4lab(t − 1)
oc3_cit1cap oc3_cit4cap	Oc3_cit1cap = 69.84 * + 0.75* oc3_cit1cap(t − 1) + 0.82 * oc3_cit4cap (t − 1) Oc3_cit4cap = 870.77* − 1.13* oc3_cit1cap (t − 1) − 0.96 * oc3_cit4cap (t − 1)

(continued)

Table 2.6 (continued)

oc3_cit1lab oc3_cit5lab	Oc3_cit1lab = 6123.54 * + 0.44 ** oc3_cit1lab(t – 1) + 0.04 oc3_cit5lab(t – 1) Oc3_cit5lab = 6025.53 + 0.01 oc3_cit1lab(t – 1) + 0.41 oc3_cit5lab(t – 1)
oc3_cit1cap oc3_cit5cap	Oc3_cit1cap = 18839.33 * – 24.06 * oc3_cit1cap(t – 1) – 97.78* oc3_cit5cap(t – 1) Oc3_cit5cap = –5869.07* + 8.20* oc3_cit1cap(t – 1) + 29.99* oc3_cit5cap(t – 1)
oc3_cit1lab oc3_cit6lab	Oc3_cit1lab = 6256.10 * + 0.07 oc3_cit1lab (t – 1) + 0.43 oc3_cit6lab(t – 1) Oc3_cit6lab = 5796.51 * + 0.58 oc3_cit1lab (t – 1) – 0.14 oc3_cit6lab(t – 1)
oc3_cit1cap oc3_cit6cap	Oc3_cit1cap = 134.18 + 0.81 oc3_cit1cap (t – 1) + 0.02 oc3_cit6cap (t – 1) Oc3_cit6cap = 429.75 * – 0.70 oc3_cit1cap (t – 1) + 0.58 oc3_cit6cap(t – 1)

Source: Charles and Sguotti (2021)

References

Akerlof, G. A., & Kranton, R. E. (2010). *Identity economics: How our identities shape our work, wages, and well-being*. Princeton University Press.

Arestis, P., Charles, A., & Fontana, G. (2013). Financialisation, the 'Great recession' and the stratification of the US labour market. *Feminist Economics, 19*(3), 152–180.

Arestis, P., Charles, A., & Fontana, G. (2014). Identity economics meets financialisation: Gender, race, and occupational stratification in the us labour market. *Cambridge Journal of Economics, 38*, 1471–1491.

Atkinson, A. B., Piketty, T., & Emmanuel, S. (2011). Top incomes in the long run of history. *Journal of Economic Literature, 49*, 3–71.

Bargawi, H., & Cozzi, G. (2017). Engendering economic recovery: Modeling alternatives to austerity in Europe. *Feminist Economics, 23*(4), 225–249.

Bertrand, M., Chugh, D., & Mullainathan, S. (2005). Implicit discrimination. *The American Economic Review, 95*, 94–98.

Blanton, R., Blanton, S., & Peksen, D. (2019). The gendered consequences of financial crises: A cross-national analysis. *Politics & Gender, 15*(4), 941–970.

Bornstein, G., Kugler, T., & Ziegelmeyer, A. (2004). Individual and group decisions in the centipede game: Are groups more "rational" players? *Journal of Experimental Social Psychology, 40*, 599–605.

Charles, A. (2011). Fairness and wages in Mexico's maquiladora industry: An empirical analysis on labour demand and the gender wage gap. *Review of Social Economy, 69*(1), 1–28.

Charles, A. (2012). *Exchange entitlement mapping: Theory and evidence*. New York.

Charles, A. (2021). Gender, financial crisis and labor markets. In K. Zimmermann (Ed.), *Handbook of labor, human resources and population economics*. Springer Cham. https://doi.org/10.1007/978-3-319-57365-6_29-1

Charles, A., & Sguotti, D. (2021). Sustainable earnings: How can herd behavior in financial accumulation feed into a resilient economic system? *Sustainability, 13*, 5776. https://doi.org/10.3390/su13115776

Charles, A., & Vujic, S. (2018). From elitist to sustainable earnings: Is there a group legitimacy in financial flows? *Global Labor Organization*, Working Paper 200, Maastricht.

Charles, A., Fontana, G., & Srivastava, A. (2011). India, China and the east Asian miracle: A human capital approach to inequalities. *Cambridge Journal of Regions, Economy and Society, 4*(1), 29–48.

Charness, G., & Sutter, M. (2012). Groups make better self-interested decisions. *Journal of Economic Perspectives, 26*, 157–176.

Crenshaw, K. W. (1989). Demarginalizing the intersection of race and sex: A black feminist critique of anti-discrimination doctrine, feminist theory and antiracist politics. *University of Chicago Legal Forum, 129*, 139–167.

Darity, W. (2005). Stratification economics: The role of intergroup inequality. *Journal of Economics and Finance, 29*, 144–153.

Darity, W. A., Jr., & Williams, R. (1985). Peddlers forever? Culture, competition, and discrimination. *The American Economic Review, 75*, 256–261.

Davis, J. B. (2011). *Individuals and identity in economics*. Cambridge University Press.

Dorling, D. (2013). *Unequal health: The scandal of our times*. Policy.

Eich, S. (2022). *The currency of politics: The political theory of money from Aristotle to Keynes*. Princeton University Press.

Elson, D. (2010). Gender and the global economic crisis in developing countries: A framework for analysis. *Gender and Development, 18*(2), 201–221.

Fitoussi, J. P., & Saraceno, F. (2010). *Inequality and macroeconomic performance*. OFCE/POLHIA, July, no 2010-13.

Floro, M., & Dymski, G. (2000). Financial crisis, gender, and power: An analytical framework. *World Development, 28*(7), 1269–1283.

Fukuda-Parr, S., Heintz, J., & Seguino, S. (2013). Critical perspectives on financial and economic crises: Heterodox macroeconomics meets feminist economics. *Feminist Economics, 19*(3), 4–31.

Galbraith, J. K. (2012). *Inequality and instability: A study of the world economy just before the great crisis*. Oxford University Press.

Grusky, D. B., & Weisshaar, K. (2014). *Social stratification: Class, race, and gender in sociological perspective* (4th ed.). Westview Press.

Hendry, D. F., & Juselius, K. (2001). Explaining cointegration analysis: Part II. *The Energy Journal, 0*, 75–120.

hooks, B. (2015). *Ain't I a woman: Black women and feminism* (2nd ed.). Routledge.

Karamessini, M., & Rubery, J. (Eds.). (2013). *Women and austerity: The economic crisis and the future for gender equality*. Routledge.

King, M., Ruggles, S., Alexander, J. T., Flood, S., Genadek, K., Schroeder, M. B., Trampe, B., & Vick, R. (2010). *Integrated public use microdata series, current population survey: Version 3.0*. Minnesota Population Center. [producer and distributor].

Kirchgässner, G., Wolters, J., & Hassler, U. (2013). Vector autoregressive processes. In G. Kirchgässner (Ed.), *Introduction to modern time series analysis; texts in business and economics* (pp. 127–154). Springer.

Lopez-Andreu, M., & Rubery, J. (2018). Austerity and women's employment trajectories in Spain and the UK: A comparison of two flexible labour markets. *Economic and Industrial Democracy*, 1–25.

Luxembourg Income Study (LIS) Database. (UK, France; April–July 2020). Luxembourg: LIS. 2020. Accessed April 15, 2020, from http://www.lisdatacenter.org

Massey, D. S. (2007). *Categorically unequal: The American stratification system*. Russell Sage Foundation New York.

Mazzucato, M. (2021). *Mission economy: A moonshot guide to changing capitalism, Allen Page*. Penguin Book.

McCall, L. (2005). The complexity of intersectionality. *Signs, 30*, 1771–1800.

Milanovic, B. (2016). *Global inequality: A new approach for the age of globalisation*. Harvard University Press.

Muehlheusser, G., Roider, A., & Wallmeier, N. (2015). Gender differences in honesty: Groups versus individuals. *Economics Letters, 128*, 25–29.

Peinado, P., & Serrano, F. (2018). Gender inequality in the labour market and the great recession. In P. Arestis & M. Sawyer (Eds.), *Inequality, international papers in political economy*. Palgrave Macmillan.

Piketty, T. (2014). *Capital in the twenty-first century*. Harvard University Press.

Piketty, T. (2019). *Capital and ideology*. Harvard University Press.

Rajan, R. (2010). *Fault lines: How hidden fractures still threaten the world economy*. Princeton University Press.

Tienda, M., & Lii, D. T. (1987). Minority concentration and earnings inequality: Blacks, Hispanics, and Asians compared. *American Journal of Sociology, 93*(1), 141–165.

Tomaskovic-Devey, D., & Skaggs, S. (1999). An establishment-level test of the statistical discrimination hypothesis. *Work and Occupations, 26*, 422–445.

Vargas, E. D., Huyser, K. R., Ybarra, V. D., Hollis, J., & Sanchez, G. R. (2018). The influence of the great recession on racial attitudes among non-Hispanic whites in the United States. *Journal of Economics, Race, and Policy, 1*, 196–203.

Walby, S. (2009). *Gender and the financial crisis*. UNESCO Paper. Accessed 06/07/2020, from http://www.lancs.ac.uk/fass/doc_library/sociology/Gender_and_financial_crisis_Sylvia_Walby.pdf

Chapter 3
Freeing the Collective Mind: Making Decisions With or Without Group Biases

Abstract This chapter shows that group membership and its associated cognitive bias within the self makes the assumption of "individual" decision-making problematic in that it creates a cognitive illusion of the "self" versus "others", when the self is in essence dynamic and relational. The consequence of such illusion is a mirror effect in resource allocation based on group bias. It makes the whole system of resource allocation entirely reliant on the arbitrary nature of human perception, which differ across individuals. Aggregating group biases at the macro-level then leads to herd behaviour which can have a positive or negative impact on resource allocation, consumption and conservation. Group dynamics can however work towards resource allocation and conservation if decisions are made without group biases at the micro-level, or if group biases are regulated at the macro level.

3.1 The Illusion of Self Vs. Others[1]

If we account for groupthink in individual-decision-making seriously, the boundaries around the self in the "self-interest" assumption become blurred. This is not to argue around altruistic vs. self-interested motives in decision-making. Rather, group membership and its associated cognitive bias within the self makes the fundamental assumption of "individual" decision-making problematic. In effect, at an ontological level, neo-classical economics is underpinned by an implicit assumption of the "essentialist self", where the self-interest of the consumer or the producer, as utility-maximiser and profit-maximiser respectively, is treated as the 'natural' and 'universal' self, and those not closely resembling one or the other are treated as 'other'. Separating the self and other results in the other being devalued and marginalised relative to the self. This is an argument developed further in Bondy and Charles (2020) around stakeholder theory and on which this section is based.

[1] This section draws from Bondy and Charles (2020).

A. Charles, *Sustainable Earnings in a Resilient Economic System*, SpringerBriefs in Economics, https://doi.org/10.1007/978-3-031-67573-7_3

Looking at the essentialist self on the basis of gender in traditional Western thinking, the concept of man is associated with autonomy, independence, and rationality, whereas the concept of woman is associated with relationships, connectedness and subjectivity (Nelson, 1997, 2014). These characteristics often hold as 'natural facts' (Flax, 1987), where men embody such things as freedom and rationality as an extension of being a man, whereas women embody such things as connectedness and interdependence as an extension of being a woman (Gilligan, 1982). Based on this view, we can understand the essence of 'man' or 'woman' through these 'natural facts'. They tell us what it means to be man or woman beyond differences in biology (Budgeon, 2014). Given that in contemporary Western societies we tend to value such characteristics as rationality and independence, over connectedness and interdependence, it allows us to legitimately prefer those embodying highly valued characteristics—men—and marginalize those with poorly valued characteristics—women (Warren, 1990). Thus the deconstruction of this essentialist view is fundamental to understanding the problematic nature of gender relations where 'man' is perceived as the 'universal, natural self' and 'woman' is devalued as 'other' (Flax, 1987).

The first problem with the essentialist self is that it does not relate to experienced utility (Fig. 1.2) as it does not reflect the lived experience of most people. With categorizations like those mentioned above, the self cannot move between sides of the dichotomy (e.g. man OR woman) without risking marginalization (Butler, 2004). For instance, transsexual and transgender people do not fit neatly into one or the other side of the dichotomy during some, or all, of their lives (Doan, 2010). It is also quite clear that not all women can be described as connected, interdependent and/or subjective, nor all men rational, independent and/or autonomous. Thus, these traits are neither 'natural' (Flax, 1987), nor demonstrative of the essence of man or woman, but reflect the social experience of the gender dichotomy. In fact, very few male individuals, for example, fit into a category that presumed 'man' to refer to white, wealthy, heterosexual and with a professional qualification. In fact, this marginalizes most of 'men' that have ever been, or are now currently alive. In this way, the essentialist view of the self marginalizes most people, leaving only an elite that is socially perceived as the 'universal' self and hence dominant within social relations.

The second key concern with the essentialist self is that it is static, setting in stone cognitive biases at the level of remembered utility and hence disconnecting the self from the individual context (see Fig. 1.6). In the gender example, once we know the essence of 'man' or 'woman', these traits are held as relevant regardless of time or context. Work on masculinity and femininity in the socialist feminist tradition has fundamentally challenged this notion (Connell, 1995). Not only has it sought to separate 'man' or 'woman' from the traits associated with particular genders, but to demonstrate that these traits belong to all genders without losing the historical context in which the traits developed (Derry, 1996). These traits, or masculine and feminine ideals, change over time in relation to each other, and therefore require an analysis of their social practice *in relation* to other practices and social change, *over time* (Schippers, 2007). Men as 'risk-takers' is a recent phenomenon that only works in relation to women as 'prudential'. Thus, the simple social dichotomy, 'man' OR 'woman', is in fact the production of changing social relations and their historical context, rather than any objective identification of core biological characteristics specific to a sex. Feminist theory thus proposes an alternative to the essentialist self, called the relational self.

3.2 Dynamic and Relational Self[2]

The concept of a relational self builds upon the idea that each self is composed of multiple, intersecting selves, that while different and sometimes in conflict, do not privilege one over another, and are constantly shaped and challenged through social relations and personal introspection within relevant contexts. This section discusses these three overlapping ideas in further detail.

3.2.1 Intersectionality and Multiple Identities

First, intersectionality depicts the self at the intersection of several identities, and not a fixed essence based on a particular biological form (Crenshaw, 1989). Rather, the self is composed of multiple, heterogeneous 'others' which combine to create a self whose meaning is in relation to the other, framed within contextual hierarchies. So instead of the 'man' OR 'woman' dichotomy, intersectionality suggests that there are multiple identities such as academic, women, mother, eco-warrior, friend, partner, social activist etc. that interweave into a whole, dynamic self that shifts and is shaped in relation to other relational selves (McCall, 2005). This is not to say that the whole self is harmonious. Rather, each identity contributes in unique ways to the heterogeneity of the self and these, sometimes, conflicting selves reflect the individual's lived experience. Intersectionality thus dismantles the assumption that all women or men are the same (Nash, 2008), but rather the self is composed of a unique combination of multiple identities interrelating through social structures and that characterize how an individual experiences her/his life.

3.2.2 Different, Not Better

Second, a relational self rejects the assumption that dichotomies presume opposites, and that opposites allow us to give a higher value to one side or the other (Butler, 2004). A relational self, with multiple intersecting identities does not presume any

[2] This section also draws from Bondy and Charles (2020).

one characteristic as more or less valuable, but as different and therefore *more or less prevalent* in different contexts. Nelson's (1992) work highlights the disproportionate value given to opposites on the gender dichotomy in the context of Western thinking, and the social relations that create and maintain it. She first argues that masculine traits are far more often viewed as positive, and feminine traits as negative. She then invites us to reflect on the positive/negative counterparts of characteristics so as to neutralize the higher/lower, better/worse types of value associated with the trait. In this way, she demonstrates that gender images are ideals based on people's imagination, collective and cultural norms, and so is the value proscribed to them. As such, they can be reconstituted as differences, rather than opposites on a dichotomy, which can thus be merged to form a heterogeneous self not ascribed to fixed, perceived attributes that privilege one over the other. The relational self therefore recognizes a unique, multi-dimensional, introspective and relational self, where no trait or identity is privileged or marginalized, and that sits at the crossroads of multiple social groups.

3.2.3 Shaped by Changing Social Relations

Third, a relational self is a self that is shaped in interaction with other relational selves, and both shapes, and is shaped by, dynamic social structures (e.g. Borgerson, 2007) that change over time and space (e.g. Charles, 2012). In other words, to understand the self, we look at the perceived attributes of others and, through introspection, form our personal identity in relation to the identities of other groups. In the latest wave of transnational feminism, the perception of social identities is context-based and founded on globalised ideals of femininity and masculinity (e.g. Pearson, 2007), as well as ideals of other social groups such as race, ethnicity, occupation, nationality etc. (e.g. Charles, 2012), that constantly evolve in relation to one another. As such, defining the self is as much about the unique composition of selves that form the whole, as it is about the way each self defines itself relative to other social groups.

Overall, the feminist contribution to the understanding of the self departs from a dualistic view based on opposites such as 'man' or 'woman', to a dynamic and relational self constantly evolving. As such, it recognizes and embraces all the multiple identities that make up a unique and heterogeneous self. In this way, the self and other are combined into a relational self through introspection and social interaction. Building from Fig. 1.6, Fig. 3.1 shows the dynamic and relational self with one identity-based entitlement, while the next Sect. 3.3 shows how such framing works in resource allocation.

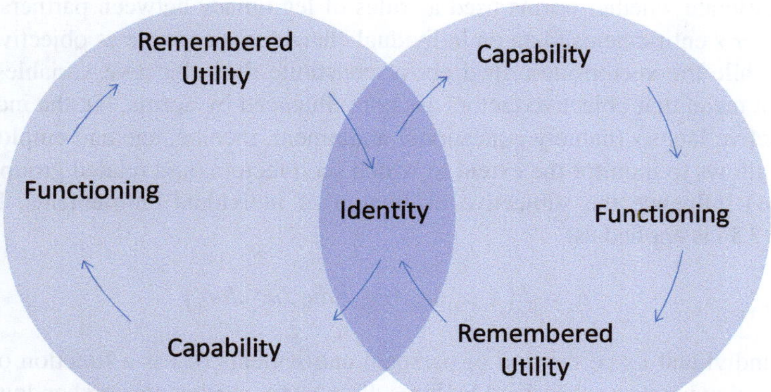

Fig. 3.1 Dynamic and Relational Self with Relational Identity-based entitlement

3.3 Implications: The Mirror Effect in Resource Allocation[3]

Placing identity at the centre of resource allocation means that, in the relational context that the social sphere offers, the extent to which individual's access to resources depends on context-based relations, one's perception of resource allocation, others' perception of one's access to resources, and the actual access to resources. Let us therefore assume a society with *m*-individuals, $i = 1,..,m$, included in *l*-households $h = 1,...,l$, each individual with an endowment set of *n*-resources, $x = 1,...,n$. Since there is an element of subjectivity in the entitlement framework with norms used as rules of legitimacy in exchange, entitlements are tied to the interaction between how individual *i* perceives his resource allocation, and how *i*'s allocation is perceived by others (i.e. social identity) and partner *j* in particular. Hence,, the entitlement model is:

$$e_{ii} = f\left(x_{ii}, x_{ij}, e_{ij}, \overline{x_i}\right) \tag{3.1}$$

with the subjective variables represented by the following vectors:

x_{ii} Individual *i*'s endowments as perceived by individual *i*
x_{ij} Individual *i*'s endowments as perceived by partner *j*
e_{ii} Individual *i*'s level of access to corresponding *x* as perceived by individual *i*
e_{ij} Individual *i*'s level of access to corresponding *x* as perceived by partner *j*;

and $\overline{x_i} \in \Re^n_+$ is a set of objective endowments of *i* such as age, income, or level of education.

---

[3] This section draws from Charles and De Pascali (2023).

To estimate whether norms used as rules of legitimacy between partners affect each other's entitlements, data on individual characteristics serve as objective variables, while the vectors described above constitute the subjective variables. This does not mean that objective factors are not influenced by norms, but the inclusion of objective factors (namely educational attainment, income, age and employment status) allows to monitor the extent to which such factors (and related group memberships) influence the subjective evaluation of individual entitlements. Hence, model (3.1) is applied as:

$$e_{ii} = f\left(x_{ii}, x_{ij}, e_{ij}, Age_i, Edu_i, Inc_i, Job_i\right) \tag{3.2}$$

where individual *i*'s perception of personal entitlements (e_{ii}) is a function of individual endowments as perceived by himself (x_{ii}), the entitlements and endowments of individual *i* as perceived by the partner *j* (e_{ij} and x_{ij} respectively), and a set of objective variables age (*Age*), education (*Edu*), income (*Inc*), and employment status (*Job*).

The method used to test the entitlement framework is to build a self-reported measure of entitlements showing the cross-perception of resource allocation between two individuals, male and female, within the household. Given that the dependent variable in Eq. (3.2) is categorical, the statistical analysis makes use of ordered logit and multinomial logistic regressions to explore the categorical nature of subjective variables vis-a-vis objective variables, and the extent to which each type of variable influences perception of resource entitlements relative to gender, within and across samples. Social identity in this research is composed of three layers of group membership embedded in a fixed geographic context chosen, namely the Mezzogiorno. The three layers of membership are in terms of a cultural group as a social construct in the two different sub-regions of Puglia and Campania, the nuclear family household as a social unit of the Christian society, and gender as a social construct of men and women's roles. Traditional gender norms in the Mezzogiorno strongly affect the work-life balance between male and female household members. The sampling target is households with a mixed-gender couple at its head to keep in line with the family model associated with the Christian background in Lecce (Puglia region) and Benevento (Campania region).

Two questions are asked for each of the 20 resources investigated. First, perceived endowments are the answers to whether the respondent owns or make use of the resource, the answer being labelled "yes" or "no". Coded 1 if yes and 0 if no, the answers for all resources represent the individual endowment vector as perceived by the individual. The respondent is then asked to repeat the exercise for the partner, thus revealing their own perception of the partner's endowments. These answers for all resources give a set of two vectors: the individual endowment vector as perceived by the individual x_{ii}, and the endowment vector of the same individual as perceived by the partner x_{ij}. Second, entitlements are the answers to whether the respondent is entitled to the resource, using the label scales "not enough", "enough" and "more than enough"—then coded 0, 1 and 2, respectively. These levels are consistent with the measurement procedures of qualitative research methods, whose distinguishing features are identity, rank order, equal intervals, and true zero points (Kahneman &

Tversky, 2013), and the use of label scales rather than rating scales allow respondents to have a clearer understanding of the scale. The answers for all resources represent the individual entitlement vector as perceived by the individual. The respondent is then asked to repeat the exercise for the partner, thus revealing his or her own perception of the entitlements of the partner. These answers for all resources give a set of two vectors as shown in Eq. (3.1): the entitlement vector of the individual as perceived by the individual e_{ii}, and the entitlement vector of the individual as perceived by the partner e_{ij}. Twenty resources describe all the major entitlements that can be expected for a good life, on the assumption that this is one definition of a good life.[4]

Despite the sampling differences, Table 3.1 shows a similar sense of ownership on average for men and women in both samples with a mean endowment of 0.63 and 0.65 for men and women respectively, in the Benevento sample, and a mean endowment of 0.62 and 0.64 for men and women, respectively, in the Lecce sample. Using intra-household panel data, the entitlement model (3.2) is estimated as follows:

$$e_{ii} = \alpha + \beta_1 x_{ii} + \beta_2 x_{ij} + \beta_3 e_{ij} + \beta_4 Age_i + \beta_5 Edu_i + \beta_6 Inc_i + \beta_7 Job_i + \varepsilon \quad (3.3)$$

where $\varepsilon IID\left(0,\sigma_\delta^2\right)$ is the error term and $\propto$ is the constant term.

The individual i's perception of personal entitlements (e_{ii}) depends on individual endowments as perceived by individual i (x_{ii}), the entitlements and endowment of i as perceived by partner j (e_{ij} and x_{ij} respectively), and objective variables including age (*Age*), education (*Edu*), income (*Inc*), and employment status (*Job*). The entitlement variables are categorical variables split according to the "not enough", "enough", and "more than enough" according to each good in x. Such categorical variables make ordered and multinomial specifications the ideal method to estimate Eq. (3.3). The model is in effect estimated on each sample, which allows us to identify regional discrepancies between the cities of Lecce and Benevento. Equation (3.3) is estimated with a multinomial regression by entitlement level and by partner, which allows us to identify, within the gender identity group, the factors affecting the entitlement levels "not enough" and "more than enough" using the level "enough" as a base outcome.

Table 3.1 Sense of ownership by gender as perceived by the gender

Sample	Gender	Mean endowment	N	Standard deviation
Benevento	Man	0.63	1218	0.481
	Woman	0.65	1201	0.476
Lecce	Man	0.62	1491	0.485
	Woman	0.64	1533	0.483

Note: *N* represents the number of resource endowments (20) multiplied by the number of respondents. A breakdown per resource is available in Charles and De Pascali (2023)

[4] For further details, see Charles and De Pascali (2023).

Using a multinomial logistic regression, model (3.3) is estimated by geographic sample (Benevento versus Lecce), and by male and female partners (i.e. men and women). The results are displayed in Table 3.2. All models are statistically significant as reflected by the WaldChi2 and LRChi2 results. Comparing men and women in both samples, the partner's perception of one's entitlements is again a significant factor to explain both "not enough" and "more than enough" levels of entitlements. If the partner's perception of one's entitlements was to improve, the multinomial log odds for "not enough" relative to "enough" entitlements would be expected to decrease by 1.17 for Benevento men, by 1.75 for Benevento women, and by 1.82 for Lecce men, while the finding is not significant for Lecce women, again. On the other hand, if the partner's perception of one's entitlements was to improve, the multinomial log odds for "more than enough" relative to "enough" entitlements

Table 3.2 Levels of entitlements with "enough" as base outcome

Dependent variable:	Benevento				Lecce			
i's entitlement according to i	Man		Woman		Man		Woman	
Not enough								
Constant	18.24	(1.02)*	16.55	(1.20)*	0.18	(1.54)	0.40	(0.15)
i's endowment according to *i*	−15.9	(0.79)*	−15.48	(0.96)*	1.43	(1.45)	−1.18	(2.21)
i's endowment according to *j*	−2.25	(0.34)*	−1.59	(0.84)**	−2.51	(1.56)	−2.62	(2.15)
i's entitlement according to *j*	−1.17	(0.62)**	−1.75	(0.28)*	−1.82	(0.59)*	0.15	(0.94)
Age	0.01	(0.01)	−0.01	(0.01)	0.02	(0.01)*	0.03	(0.15)*
Education	0.08	(0.10)	0.09	(0.13)	0.31	(0.17)	−0.14	(0.13)
Income	−0.13	(0.10)	0.01	(0.07)	−0.26	(0.07)*	−0.37	(0.13)*
Job	−0.57	(0.23)*	0.37	(0.29)	0.03	(1.54)	0.07	(0.04)**
More than enough:								
Constant	12.95	(1.62)*	13.52	(1.72)*	−6.41	(2.03)*	0.16	(1.36)
i's endowment according to *i*	−15.4	(0.46)*	−14.11	(1.19)*	4.43	(2.03)*	−0.62	(1.38)
i's endowment according to *j*	0.46	(0.78)	−1.03	(1.34)	−3.11	(2.07)	−3.12	(2.24)
i's entitlement according to *j*	1.88	(0.37)*	1.44	(0.32)*	2.54	(0.49)*	1.08	(0.81)
Age	−0.01	(0.02)	−0.04	(0.04)*	0.00	(0.01)	−0.01	(0.10)
Education	0.17	(0.15)	0.12	(0.17)	0.16	(0.20)	0.02	(0.21)
Income	−0.19	(0.11)**	0.09	(0.11)	0.25	(0.12)*	0.14	(0.13)
Job	−0.64	(0.55)	−0.72	(0.42)**	−0.01	(0.05)	−0.01	(0.04)
Number of observations	580	565			862		727	
LRChi2(16) or WaldChi2(14)	2399*	1390*			159.64*		75.06*	
Pseudo R-square	0.26	0.18			0.11		0.07	

Note: Robust standard errors in brackets are adjusted for correlation of answers belonging to each individual; *and ** mean that the coefficient is significant at the 5% and 10% level, respectively. Standard errors are adjusted clusters in the household variable would be expected to increase by 1.88 for Benevento men, by 1.44 for Benevento women, and by 2.54 for Lecce men, while the finding is not significant for Lecce women. The single most important factor for Lecce women is access to income, whereby if women were to have access to a higher income category, the multinomial log odds for "not enough" relative to "enough" entitlements would be expected to decrease by 0.37. In other words, access to higher income would improve entitlement levels for Lecce women, more than any other factor in the model. Finally, comparing the relationality of gender between both samples, for the level "not enough", all the subjective variables are statistically significant for the Benevento sample and none are for the Lecce sample, where the lack of income is the main relevant factor for both men and women.

To appreciate the dynamics at play in the findings, the above-mentioned results are shown diagrammatically in Figs. 3.2 and 3.3. Figure 3.2 maps the results for men and women in Benevento and men in Lecce due to the similar outcome that "identity" derived from remembered utility is at the heart of resource allocation, as shown in Fig. 3.1. In Fig. 3.3 however, the results for women in Lecce show that the availability of resources is at the heart of resource allocation, regardless of identity, which suggests that experienced utility is the basis of resource entitlement for them.

First of all, the results show that gender relations are context-based (1) since, even within the same geographic context of the Mezzogiorno, localised differences in the gender identity emerged between Benevento and Lecce. Second, the results confirm that one's perception of resource allocation (2) is shaped by (1), (3) and (4), with positive or negative impact on personal identity. Finally, while the actual access to resources (4) gives a similar sense of endowments across both samples (Table 3.1), the way it influences one's perception of resource allocation (2) differs between Figs. 3.2 and 3.3. In Fig. 3.2, for men and women in Benevento and men in Lecce,

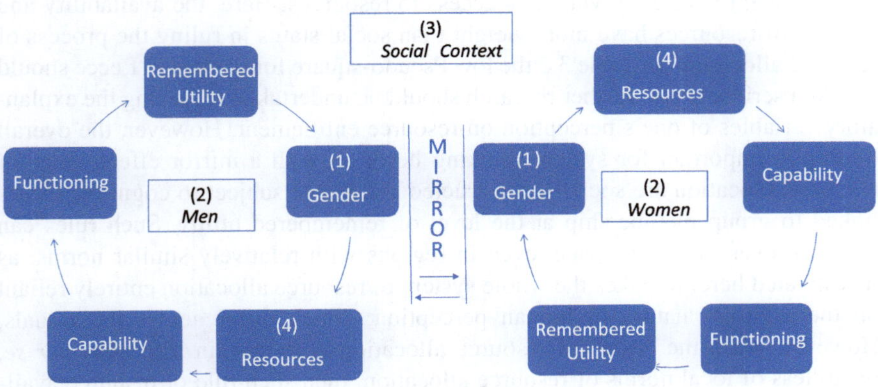

Fig. 3.2 The mirror effect in resource entitlement for men and women in Benevento and men in Lecce

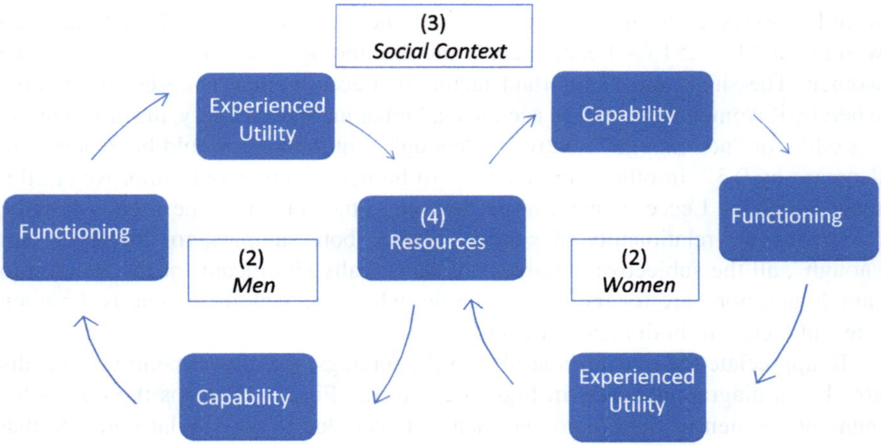

Fig. 3.3 Resource entitlement based on experienced utility for women in Lecce

the connection of the individual to the social context is via the relational gender identity (1), which then determines one's access to resources (4). Here, the social rules of legitimacy in access to resources rule the process of resource allocation. As such, the proposition is that there is *a mirror effect in resource entitlements* whereby one's resource entitlements is based on others' resource entitlements rather than on his or her actual access to resources. In simple terms, it means that "what you have/have not" reflects on "what I consider to have/have not" regardless of resource availability.

In Fig. 3.3 however, for women in Lecce, the connection of the individual to the social context is directly via one's access to resources. Here, the availability and scarcity of resources have more weight than social status in ruling the process of resource allocation. In Table 3.2 the low Pseudo-square for women in Lecce should be taken seriously and further research should be undertaken regarding the explanatory variables of one's perception on resource entitlement. However, the overall finding is important for system thinking because, with a mirror effect, rules of resource allocation are socially constructed and hence subject to cognitive biases linked to group membership at the level of remembered utility. Such rules can fluctuate over time and space, even in regions with relatively similar norms, as investigated here. It makes the whole system of resource allocation entirely reliant on the arbitrary nature of human perception, which differ across individuals. However, when the "rule" of resource allocation is to sustain resources *per se*, regardless of local norms of resource allocation, then such rule of resource availability and conservation can maximise the survival of the whole system. Such viewpoint has long been put forward by the work of Elinor Ostrom, as will be discussed now.

3.4 Freeing the Collective Mind: With or Without Group Biases?

With a mirror effect, the self keeps the illusion of making decisions freely when it is actually based on remembered utility where the comfort of group biases lies, among other cognitive biases. It is comfortable in the sense that it reduces the uncertainty linked to life choices when decision-making then relies more on the perceived boundaries of group membership (such as group preferences or characteristics) than on life experience at the point of experienced utility. Consequently, the perception of life at the point of remembered utility is tainted through the lens of group biases, bounced back through the mirror effect. It then leads to herd behaviour in the way group biases per individual aggregate in a cumulative fashion. Herd behaviour then have a positive or negative impact on resource allocation, consumption and conservation. The question now is whether individual freedom of choice is just an illusion in the context of group biases. In effect, let me reframe the question to whether "freedom" of choice with group bias is a valid basis for "individual" decision-making, or is it rather an illusion of individual freedom. If so, then alleviating group biases can free the collective mind of the potential negative impact they have on resource allocation, consumption and conservation.

To understand how to alleviate group biases in individual and collective decision-making, we will now look at potential positive and negative impacts of group behaviour. So far, in Chaps. 1 and 2, we have looked at "negative" examples of herd behaviour. Relevant examples have included the demographics of discrimination in financial accumulation in Western economies (Darity, 2005; Arestis et al., 2014; Charles, 2021), but it also extends to inter-group conflicts worldwide (Stewart, 2008), herd-behaviour on global demand with the example of the consumption of textiles leading to water depletion in China (Li et al., 2017). Positive examples of herd-behaviour include numerous social movements that led to positive societal and environmental changes such as the movement leading to the widespread use of bicycles in the Netherlands, the Fridays For Future movement, or the #MeToo and #BlackLivesMatter movements globally.

Those examples, both positive and negative, illustrate the fact that the impact herd-behaviour is not predictable. At the micro-level, cognitive mechanisms of group biases affect remembered utility which serves as a basis for decision-making. This means that there is a propensity for the narrative of dominant groups to be imposed on the rest of the world. And, as witnessed by colonisation regimes on the land and sea, dominance is a proxy for ownership (Charles & Blondel, 2023). Hence, at the macro-level, the cumulative effect of group biases leads both to a distortion of resource allocation towards dominant groups, but also to the deterioration of natural resources that herd-behaviour brings, as witnessed by the Great Acceleration.

Given the intersection of group biases, it is however difficult to predict the different trends of herd behaviour, unless we are already aware, to a certain extent, of the current trends in inequality between groups (which we will see in the next Chapter on the concept of Sustainable Earnings). The question raised however here is: what would happen if decisions were taken at the level of experienced utility similarly to Fig. 3.3? Would there be any group biases as a result? Would group bias still aggregate to distort resource allocation? And if so, what sort of group mechanisms could work towards resource allocation and conservation? Let's explore each level of analysis in turn to assess the impact of decisions made at the point of experienced utility at micro-level, and whether it would alleviate group biases at the macro level.

3.4.1 Micro-level: The Power of the Local Context

At the micro-level, Fig. 3.4 builds from Fig. 1.2 to show the role of the ecological context in an individual's decision-making process with group biases. At the point of experienced utility, the ecological context shapes the way individuals experience the world. Then, group biases reshape experienced utility through a cognitive process that disconnects the individual from their ecological context. Decisions are then made at the point of remembered utility, affected by group biases, and the revealed preferences resulting from this decision-making process show in the ecological context, bearing the mark of cognitive biases. Group biases therefore disconnect decision-making the actual experience of the ecological context.

One notable example of the positive environmental impact of group behaviour is based on Ostrom's work on governing the commons and her principles for managing Common Pool Resources (CPR) (Ostrom, 1990). In effect, the majority of the eight design principles of CPR management present a strong element of group membership that eventually enables, in the local context, to preserve natural resources effectively in the long run. Ostrom's eight design principles reproduced in Table 3.3 are namely: (1) clear boundaries and memberships, (2) congruent rules,

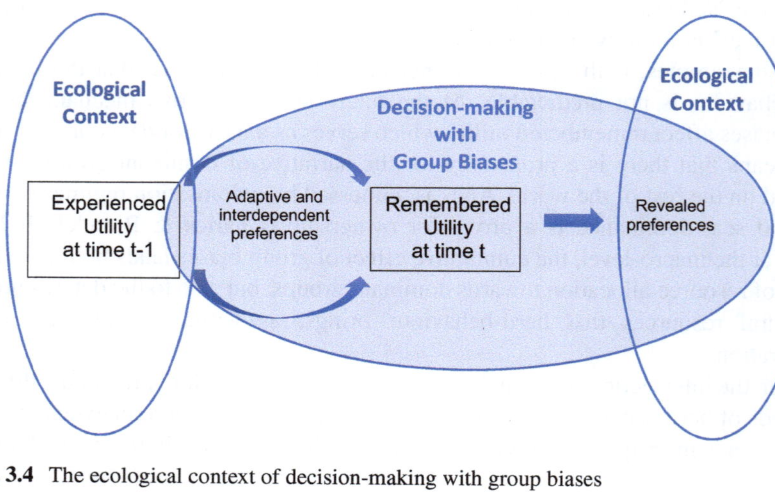

Fig. 3.4 The ecological context of decision-making with group biases

Table 3.3 Design principles and institutional performance, Ostrom (1990: 180)

Site	(1) Clear boundaries and memberships	(2) Congruent rules	(3) Collective choice arenas	(4) Monitoring	(5) Graduated sanctions	(6) Conflict resolution mechanisms	(7) Recognized rights to organize	(8) Nested units	Institutional performance
Törbel, Switzerland	Yes	Yes	Yes	Yes	Yes	Yes	Yes	NR[a]	Robust
Japanese mountain villages	Yes	Yes	Yes	Yes	Yes	Yes	Yes	NR	Robust
Valencia, Murcia, and Oriheula, Spain	Yes	Yes	Yes	Yes	Yes	Yes	Yes	Yes	Robust
Raymond, West and Central basins (current)	Yes	Yes	Yes	Yes	Yes	Yes	Yes	Yes	Robust
Alicante, Spain	Yes	Yes	Yes	Yes	Yes	Yes	Yes[b]	Yes	Robust
Bacarra-Vintar, Philippines	Yes	Yes	Yes	Yes	Yes	Yes	Yes	Yes	Robust
Alanya, Turkey	No	Yes	Weak	Yes	Yes	Weak	Weak	NR	Fragile
Gal Oya, Sri Lanka	Yes	Yes	Yes	Yes	[c]	Weak	Weak	Yes	Fragile
Port Lameron, Canada	Yes	Yes	Weak	Yes	Yes	Yes	No	No	Fragile
Bay of Izmir and Bodrum, Turkey	No	No	No	No	No	No	Weak	No	Failure
Mawelle, Sri Lanka	No	Yes	No	Yes	Yes	No	No	No	Failure
Kirindi Oya, Sri Lanka	Yes	No	No	No	No	No	No	No	Failure

(continued)

Table 3.3 (continued)

Site	(1) Clear boundaries and memberships	(2) Congruent rules	(3) Collective choice arenas	(4) Monitoring	(5) Graduated sanctions	(6) Conflict resolution mechanisms	(7) Recognized rights to organize	(8) Nested units	Institutional performance
Raymond, West, and Central basins (earlier)	No	No	No	No	No	Yes	Yes	No	Failure
Mojave groundwater basins	No	No	Yes	No	No	Yes	Yes	No	Failure

[a] NR = not relevant
[b] With two major exceptions, from 1739 to 1840 and 1930 to 1950
[c] Missing information

(3) collective choice arenas, (4) monitoring, (5) graduated sanctions, (6) conflict-resolution mechanism, (7) recognised rights to organise and (8) nested units. Principles (1), (2), (4) and (5) are present in the eight sites with no institutional failures, and they all relate to strong group membership and its associated norms of behaviour to effectively manage the commons locally.

The design principles (1), (2), (4) and (5) are behavioural rules engrained at the level of remembered utility for individuals in the sites investigated and they have been so for hundreds of years in some cases. However, while such community-led management systems are powerful in making use of norms and group behaviour, it is not clear how such mechanisms can be scaled-up at a regional, national or global level of resource allocation. In effect, while the strength of group membership in Ostrom's framework relies on group membership designed around resource conservation, once market exchange takes place, the financial transaction breaks the cognitive link between decision-making and the local context.

In market exchange, group membership removes the "self" from their context of decision-making, or experienced utility, and uses the boundaries of group membership instead as a basis for decision-making, or in other words remembered utility. Such cognitive process removes the cognitive link of decision-making from the ecological context and potential ecological impact of market decisions. The ecological context of decision-making however matters, and ecological rationality has long argued that the context in which decision-making takes place influences the outcome decision and its environmental impact (Gigerenzer & Todd, 1999). This makes community-based initiatives such as the ones studied by Ostrom successful in conserving natural resources and embracing local priorities in a way that preserve that cognitive link to the ecological context.

Promoting group membership around local resource use can be illustrated by numerous other examples of community-led interventions that have been successful in resource conservation (Krasny et al., 2011). Examples include the community-led initiatives triggered by the theoretical framework of Doughnut Economics (Raworth, 2017), but also civil society organisations pushing for sustainable development (Asia Civil Society Partnership for Sustainable Development, Arab NGO Network for Development, or the Pacific Islands Association of NGOs), and the numerous coastal community-based initiatives for ocean conservation (Charles & Blondel, 2023). Finally, there is now a widespread recognition that indigenous knowledge is vital for the local implementation of the SDGs (Global Sustainable Development Report, 2023). In the light of such locally-based initiatives, the future promises to be made of islands of excellence in resource conservation, while the allocation of resources in between may or may not remain prone to herd-behaviour, as we will now see.

3.4.2 *Macro-level: Aggregating and Alleviating Group Biases*

In Western economies, at the macro-level, we have seen in Chap. 3 that there is now a two-tier system where, at the top of the income distribution, financialisation led to "financing finance" (Mazzucato, 2021) going in the hands of a few dominant groups, while leaving labour earners with stagnant real-wages in the second tier. Domination here is again used as a proxy for ownership, similarly to maritime colonisation regimes (Charles & Blondel, 2023), or at least the illusion of ownership through the lens of group bias leading to the real control of resources.

Tackling the negative impact of group biases means that policy interventions should re-allocate resources to alleviate such negative impact while promoting the positive impact of group biases. For pro-environmental behaviour for example, we know that the types of interventions influencing the choice made by individuals, the so-called "downstream" interventions such as information, advertising, education and social approaches, tend to be 2–3% effective. Meanwhile, the so-called "upstream" interventions influencing the context of decision-making such as economic policy, nudges, regulations and changes to built environment tend to be up to 100% effective (Nisa et al., 2019; Verplanken & Wood, 2006). This confirms the importance of ecological rationality to account for context in policy-making, but it also begs the question as to why influencing individual choices are not so effective.

To be effective in market exchange, downstream interventions need to promote decision-making at the point of experienced utility where the cognitive link to the ecological context of decision may still be alive. We see it in the way that paying for a resource often removes the individual's responsibility from the impact of its consumption. A concrete example is the illusion that carbon markets create by issuing a license to pollute instead of cutting for carbon emissions in absolute terms. Instead, downstream interventions should first identify the boundaries of group memberships involved in market exchange by gathering data on group membership, and then targeting the responsibility of individual behaviour by showing the link between individual and group behaviour on the one hand, and showing the link between the group's revealed preferences and its environmental impact on the other hand. If not effective in targeting experienced utility, then downstream interventions in market exchange should target remembered utility directly, re-allocating resources systemically so as to remove the cognitive biases affecting negatively resource allocation, and encouraging cognitive biases affecting resource allocation positively. For example, gradual taxes on frequent flyers based on Ostrom's graduated sanctions principle, alongside subsidies for low-carbon travellers could be effective in alleviating group biases and in promoting positive change.

3.5 Conclusion

Overall, this Chapter has shown that group membership and its associated cognitive bias within the self makes the assumption of "individual" decision-making problematic in that it creates a cognitive illusion of the "self" versus "others", when the self is in essence dynamic and relational. The consequence of such illusion is a mirror effect in resource allocation based on group bias. It makes the whole system of resource allocation entirely reliant on the arbitrary nature of human perception, which differ across individuals. Aggregating group biases at the macro-level then leads to herd behaviour which can have a positive or negative impact on resource allocation, consumption and conservation. Group dynamics can however work towards resource allocation and conservation if decisions are made without group biases at the micro-level, or if group biases are regulated at the macro level. The next Chapter proposes the concept of sustainable earnings to show how group biases at the macro level could be alleviated or encouraged for a resilient economic system able to channel finance towards sustainable goals.

References

Arestis, P., Charles, A., & Fontana, G. (2014). Identity economics meets financialisation: Gender, race, and occupational stratification in the us labour market. *Cambridge Journal of Economics, 38*, 1471–1491.

Bondy, K., & Charles, A. (2020). Mitigating stakeholder marginalisation with the relational self. *Journal of Business Ethics, 165*, 67–82. https://doi.org/10.1007/s10551-018-4085-x

Borgerson, J. L. (2007). On the harmony of feminist ethics and business ethics. *Business and Society Review, 112*(4), 477–509.

Budgeon, S. (2014). The dynamics of gender hegemony: Femininities, masculinities and social change. *Sociology, 48*(2), 317–334.

Butler, J. (2004). *Undoing gender*. Routledge.

Charles, A. (2012). *Exchange entitlement mapping: Theory and evidence*. New York.

Charles, A. (2021). Gender, financial crisis and labor markets. In K. Zimmermann (Ed.), *Handbook of labor, human resources and population economics*. Springer Cham. https://doi.org/10.1007/978-3-319-57365-6_29-1

Charles, A., & Blondel, P. (Eds.). (2023). Our oceans: A deep dive. *Institute for Policy Research Report*. https://doi.org/10.5281/zenodo.7736214

Charles, A., & De Pascali, P. (2023). The Mirror effect in resource entitlements: Evidence from Italian households. Available at SSRN. https://doi.org/10.2139/ssrn.4407547

Connell, R. (1995). *Masculinities*. Polity Press.

Crenshaw, K. W. (1989). Demarginalizing the intersection of race and sex: A black feminist critique of anti-discrimination doctrine, feminist theory and antiracist politics. *University of Chicago Legal Forum, 129*, 139–167.

Darity, W. (2005). Stratification economics: The role of intergroup inequality. *Journal of Economics and Finance, 29*, 144–153.

Derry, R. (1996). Toward a feminist firm: Comments on John Dobson and Judith White. *Business Ethics Quarterly, 6*(1), 101–109.

Doan, P. L. (2010). The tyranny of gendered spaces – Reflections from beyond the gender dichotomy. *Gender, Place and Culture, 17*(5), 635–654.

Flax, J. (1987). Postmodernism and gender relations in feminist theory. *Signs, 12*(4), 621–643.

Gigerenzer, G., & Todd, P. M. (1999). Ecological rationality: The normative study of heuristics. In G. Gigerenzer, P. M. Todd, & The ABC Research Group (Eds.), *Ecological rationality: Intelligence in the world* (pp. 487–497). Oxford University Press.

Gilligan, C. (1982). *In a different voice*. Harvard University Press.

Global Sustainable Development Report (GSDR). (2023). *Times of crisis, times of change: Science for accelerating transformations to sustainable development*. Independent Group of Scientists appointed by the Secretary-General, United Nations, New York.

Kahneman, D., & Tversky, A. (2013). Choices, values, and frames. In L. C. MacLean & W. T. Ziemba (Eds.), *Handbook of the fundamentals of financial decision making: Part I* (pp. 269–278). World Scientific Handbook in financial Economic Series.

Krasny, M. E., Lundholm, C., & Plummer, R. (Eds.). (2011). *Resilience in Social-Ecological Systems: The Role of Learning and Education* (1st ed.). Routledge. https://doi.org/10.4324/9781315868387

Li, Y., Lu, L., Tan, Y., Wang, L., & Shen, M. (2017). Decoupling water consumption and environmental impact on textile industry by using water footprint method: A case study in China. *Water, 9*, 124. https://doi.org/10.3390/w9020124

Mazzucato, M. (2021). *Mission economy: A moonshot guide to changing capitalism, Allen Page*. Penguin Book.

McCall, L. (2005). The complexity of intersectionality. *Signs, 30*, 1771–1800.

Nash, J. C. (2008). Re-thinking intersectionality. *Feminist Review, 89*, 1–15.

Nelson, J. (1992). Thinking about gender. *Hypatia, 7*(3), 138–154.

Nelson, J. A. (1997). Feminist, ecology and the philosophy of economics. *Ecological Economics, 20*, 155–162.

Nelson, J. A. (2014). The power of stereotyping and confirmation bias to overwhelm accurate assessment: The case of economics, gender, and risk aversion. *Journal of Economic Methodology, 21*(3), 211–231.

Nisa, C. F., Bélanger, J. J., Schumpe, B. M., et al. (2019). Meta-analysis of randomised controlled trials testing behavioural interventions to promote household action on climate change. *Nature Communications, 10*, 4545. https://doi.org/10.1038/s41467-019-12457-2

Ostrom, E. (1990). *Governing the commons: The evolution of institutions for collective action*. Cambridge University Press.

Pearson, R. (2007). Beyond women workers: Gendering CSR. *Third World Quarterly, 28*(4), 731–749.

Raworth, K. (2017). *Doughnut economics: Seven ways to think like a 21st-century economist*. Chelsea Green Publishing.

Schippers, M. (2007). Recovering the feminine other: Masculinity, femininity, and gender hegemony. *Theory and Society, 36*(1), 85–102.

Stewart, F. (Ed.). (2008). *Horizontal inequalities and conflict: Understanding group violence in multiethnic societies*. Palgrave Macmillan.

Verplanken, B., & Wood, W. (2006). Interventions to break and create consumer habits. *Journal of Public Policy & Marketing, 25*(1), 90–103. https://doi.org/10.1509/jppm.25.1.90

Warren, K. (1990). The power and promise of ecological feminism. *Environmental Ethics, 12*(3), 125–146.

Chapter 4
Sustainable Earnings for a Resilient Economic System

Abstract What makes an economic system resilient? It is one that first recognises the role of group behaviour in financial accumulation and manages to redirect its excesses where needed. This Chapter therefore look at the bubbling effect of group accumulation affecting the resilience of the entire system of financial flows, before describing how to improve the fluidity and resilience of the system. Applying such understanding to the Sustainable Development Goals, I then go on to look at the local and national governance systems necessary to facilitate a fluid and resilient system or resource and financial flows. Whether improving the fluidity and resilience of the entire system of financial flows occur would depend on taking 'groupism' rather than 'individualism' seriously in policy-making. Ironically enough, it is also an individual task for each of us to go back to the point of experienced utility in decision-making: sensing the ecological context of decision-making to trigger the individual responsibility of one's ecological footprint.

4.1 Introduction

At the COP28 in Dubai in 2023, world leaders agreed to move away from fossil fuels. It is now imperative that the world moves beyond the traditional fossil fuel metrics of economic output epitomised by GDP if the pledge to move away from oil, coal and gas is to become a reality. GDP is a measure of material production, which means that the continued use of GDP as a beacon for economic policies is holding back global sustainable development efforts. Can the world phase out fossil fuels without changing its metrics? The SDGs certainly allow us to retain the old GDP metric (SDG8) to keep track of material output, while monitoring progress to stay within planetary boundaries. The momentum to abandon 'GDP fetishism' is not new. But, while efforts to replace the GDP metric have been numerous, ultimately GDP growth is the prevalent metric reported and targeted in economic policies. It however sustains a fictional narrative of eternal growth from an old world tainted by the lens of a perceived Western dominance, while the rest of the world has already embraced the reality of systemic progress with cooperation between and

A. Charles, *Sustainable Earnings in a Resilient Economic System*,
SpringerBriefs in Economics, https://doi.org/10.1007/978-3-031-67573-7_4

across countries. Focusing on GDP as a measure for economic progress means that economic policies aiming at tackling climate change focus on the material footprint of consumption and production, as showcased by Net-zero policy pledges which have blossomed over the past few years.

The current global challenges of the Triple planetary crisis (UNEP, 2020), namely pollution, climate change and biodiversity loss however require moving away from a linear view of human ecological footprint to a systemic approach to stay within our planetary boundaries. So how to move from a linear GDP perspective, from input to output, to a systemic perspective, with synergies and trade-off within and across SDGs? One potential answer developed in this Chapter is that it can be achieved by mapping groupthink in social-ecological systems (Ostrom, 2009), locally governed through community-based SDG priorities, protected by General Average risk management mechanisms, and resourced through regional, national and international flows in a resilient economic system. As explained throughout the book, one major risk with resource (including financial) flows is for them to be exposed to groupthink phenomena that distort their impact over time towards unsustainable patterns of consumption, production, and financial accumulation. To alleviate such problem, Chap. 3 has described how a locally based management structure of social-ecological systems (Ostrom, 1990, 2009) makes a virtuous use of group norms, while aggregating group biases at the macro-level just exacerbate the momentum of resource distortion. As such, sustainable trends of capital and labour earnings would need to focus on sustaining life by nurturing a resilient system or resource allocation. Such system would imply that bubbles of *cumulative earnings should be able to be freed from groupthink* and be able to target areas where resources are needed following external shocks caused by climate change. Before presenting such system, the first section looks at the current trends in capital earnings and the possibility for them to remain business-as-usual, tainted by patterns of group-based cumulative earnings. Herd-behaviour on financial accumulation and consumption patterns have shown the dark side of the Great Acceleration so the question raised is: can groupthink have a virtuous role and be part of the solution for the Great Transition? How can group biases bridge the gap between individual decision-making and collective action? In the second section, we therefore look at the bubbling effect of group accumulation affecting the resilience of the entire system of financial flows, before describing how to improve the fluidity and resilience of the system. Finally, the last section looks at the local and national governance systems necessary to be able to facilitate a fluid and resilient system or resource flows.

4.2 Business-as-Usual Earning Trends

In Chap. 2, and Tables 2.3 and 2.4 in particular, we saw how labour and capital earnings can exhibit a cumulative pattern by group. Looking ahead, business-as-usual earning trends will lead to similar patterns of earning accumulation based on group norms, the rules of the game for financial resources allocation and hence financial flows over time. If one look at today's flows, who owns global capital which feeds into capital earnings? And similarly on the labour share of global income, what is the current trend in labour earnings? Starting with labour earnings, the post COVID-19 era provides a bleak picture. Global real wages have experienced a negative growth rate of −0.9% in the first half of 2022, which was the first time that real wages experienced negative growth in the twenty-first century (ILO, 2022). In the context of climate change, stagnant real wages at the bottom of the global income distribution leads to even more fragile livelihoods for vulnerable populations, especially those with limited access to social protection. As shown by the evidence gathered by Nesbitt-Ahmed (2023), social protection tools such as pure cash transfers or conditional cash transfers are still missing group-based criteria such as gender-responsive and age-responsive instruments to be able to channel finance where it is most needed. In effect, women, children and the elderly are the most vulnerable groups in the face of climate-related disasters, which is why more socio-demographic mapping and tailor-made policy at the group level need to be implemented and financed through public finance or public-private partnerships, before the profit-maximising intents take over socio-ecological needs, such as non-commercially viable insurance schemes for the poor.

Stagnant real wages at the bottom of the global income distribution go hand-in-hand with increasing capital earnings at the top of the income distribution in the financialisation process of global economic integration. A recent study by Gibadullina (2023) provides a comprehensive mapping of the ascent of asset manager capitalism in the US and the types of shareholders owning global capital. The ascent of asset manager capitalism means that the Big Three, namely BlackRock, Vanguard, and State Street now account for 80%–90% of all assets under management in U.S. passive equity (Gibadullina, 2023). Looking at the current trends in Gibadullina (2023), the evolution of capital ownership in the US feeds into the above mentioned two-tier system whereby the share of pension and retirement funds of the managerial and financial occupations has picked in the 1980s at 27.1%, while the share of households and non-profit ownership is collapsing from the second world war onward, although the latest still represents the major share across all types of stakeholders. The future trend looks to be linked to non-US investors whose share is rising steadily since the 2000s, with a slight resurgence in the share of households and nonprofits ownership since 2019. Outside of the US however, Bonizzi and Kaltenbrunner (2024) show that the influence of asset management is not prevalent in emerging economies. The average of the Big Three's ownership in nationally listed companies is around 2.1% only, in countries ranging from South Africa to the Czech Republic. The thorough analysis of Bonizzi and Kaltenbrunner (2024) concludes that asset managers do not seem to influence and dominate emerging markets yet, whether it is at the level of the boardroom or at the level of national macroeconomic policy.

While there is no sufficient available time-series data to map the demographics of capital ownership globally, nor there is enough data to map the demographic patterns of capital accumulation globally, the current patterns of capital ownership and accumulation show us a new trend. Yes, there is an obvious lack of finance going towards non-Western countries, as we can see through the meagre contributions of Western economies to the Loss and Damage Fund agreed at the COP28 meetings. Similarly, the SDG financing gap has surged to $3.5 trillion following the 2019 COVID crisis, with a sudden fall in external private finance of $700 billion, including a decline of 80 percent in net investment inflows, 35 percent in Foreign Direct Investment (FDI) and 20 percent in remittances (Mazzucato, 2023). Consequently, in 2023, at the halfway point of the SDG agenda for 2030, very little progress has been made in terms of a transformative reorientation of political systems and societies (Biermann et al., 2023). However, the lack of finance and the lack of political will give way to more policy space for non-Western economies to implement the SDGs according to local priorities. Many countries in the Global South have already taken the initiative to adopt and integrate progress towards the SDGs in their development plans. In Mexico for example more that 83% of 584 expenditure programs have been successfully linked to the SDGs, while in Colombia, 89% of government budget is matched to the SDGs in addition to Overseas Development Aid and private finance (Guariso et al., 2023). But due to the systemic nature of the SDGs, adopting them as a compass for economic policies would require both transparency and cooperation across public and private stakeholders globally. Mazzucato's proposition is that the SDG financing gap of seven trillion annually today be financed through mission-oriented development banks and public-private partnerships (Mazzucato, 2023). It is a sum that indeed goes beyond the financial capacity of most individual nations.

The Global South has shown a way forward by relying increasingly on South-South Cooperation initiatives. Cuban medical expertise, for example, played a crucial role in containing the Ebola outbreak in West African countries. The mission helped save hundreds of lives and prevent the further spread of the epidemic (SDG 3). Significant progress was also achieved on the goal of reaching zero hunger (SDG 2), gender equality (SDG5), decent work and economic growth (SDG8) and sustainable partnerships (SDG 17) thanks to the World Food Programme triangular cooperation with Brazil, South Africa and the Republic of Congo to tackle chronic malnutrition and find ways to help farmers make a decent living. The Global North however is lagging behind the Global South's leadership in terms of progress towards the SDGs and towards using the SDGs to measure economic progress. In producing a Voluntary National Review of the SDGs in 2019 only, the UK has not published one since. Similarly, the US has been one of the slowest countries in the OECD to align its development efforts with the SDGs, despite being a long-standing and leading actor in the creating the SDG Architecture.

So how do we align current financial flows towards sustainable goals? If we were to learn from past trends and take the reality of group behaviour seriously, the group-based demographics of current global wealth and income accumulation will inform the potential future scenarios for capital and labour earnings. Are the current patterns of group accumulation sustainable? If sustainability is understood as a self-sustaining process of earning accumulation, then the current tacit rules on group membership and associated group biases are certainly self-sustainable and financing finance for the top of a two-tier system. However, if sustainability is understood as the extent to which current earnings feed into a resilient economic system able to feed the financial needs of sustaining life on Earth, then no. There is a need to build a resilient economic system based on the norms of cooperation promoted by the Global South.

4.3 Ecological Mapping: Sustainable Earning Trends

The evidence presented throughout the book shows the extent to which group behaviour overtakes individual motives in the way resources flow between individuals. This is especially visible in the financial sector due to the magnitude of the flows in that sector, but it is a phenomenon consistent across the economy and society; from consumers as social-status seekers to online influencers and bit coins hoarders. Such a wide phenomenon raises the question whether group behaviour earnings can ever become "sustainable" in order to feed into the green transition without leading to even more greenwashing practices. "Sustainability" here is defined as the "Pursuit of Life" (Dahlmann, 2024) enabling to maintain life within our social-ecological systems with enough biodiversity to survive and, at the level of the society, enough financial resources to sustain the livelihoods of all groups rather than letting financial flows freely float towards dominant groups.

The proposition made here is that the fluidity in group relationships is key to the stability of the overall economic system. In a global network of resource flows, "[e]fficiency occurs when a system streamlines and simplifies its resource flow to achieve its aims, say by channelling resources directly between the larger nodes. Resilience, however, depends upon diversity and redundancy in the network, which means that there are ample alternative connections and options in times of shock and change." (Raworth, 2017: 175). In a global network of financial flows, each node represents a group linked to these financial flows. With groups rather than individuals at the centre of financial interactions, we can frame the entitlement rules of financial flows between the nodes. Then, any external shock on one node could be offset by other nodes around, allowing resources to move freely, free from groupthink which leads to bubbling effects that undermine the diversity and redundancy of the entire system.

Figure 4.1 illustrates a network of financial flows around one particular group in the centre, whose size and signs of past earnings positively impact on present earnings, whereby groupthink is leading to an absorption of earnings from the nodes adjacent to it. In Chap. 2, Table 2.3 gives an example of the potential signs of the relationship between past and present earnings across groups, from negative to non-significant and then positive. Overtime, the bubbling effect necroses the node and takes from the rest of the system, affecting the ecological fluidity and health of the entire system. From this perspective, a resilient system of financial flows is a healthy and fluid system of financial relationships between groups, channelling finance to

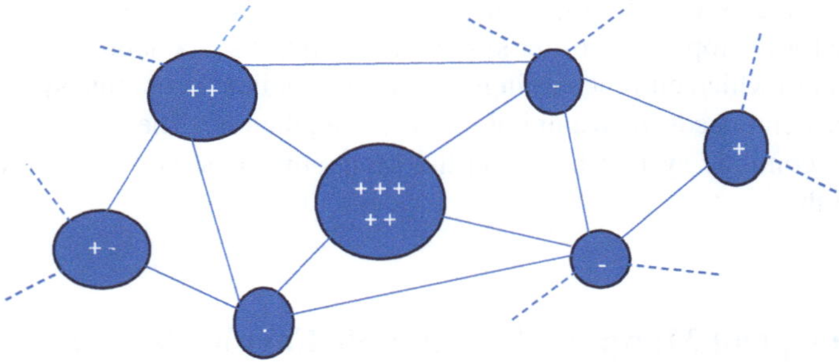

Fig. 4.1 A bubbling effect affecting the resilience of financial flows

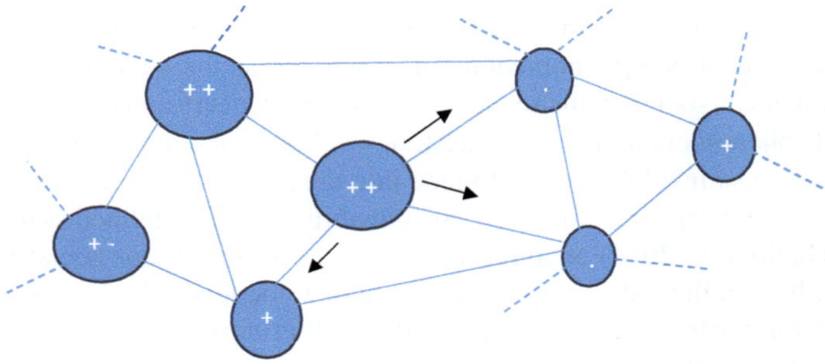

Fig. 4.2 Improving the fluidity and resilience of financial flows

sustain the fluidity of the entire system in the event of external shocks on a particular node.

In Fig. 4.2, improvements to the fluidity and resilience of the entire system are made through micro-level or macro-level interventions, alleviating the group biases in financial accumulation, and channelling finance towards groups with negative (with a negative sign) or non-significant (with a dot) links to the entire system. As such, the arrows point towards the redistribution process from Figs. 4.1 to 4.2 which allows the whole system to survive.

Building policy tools able to map out group earnings from the past will be able to inform future policies of the potential cognitive biases brought about by group behaviour at the micro-level. It also allows to raise awareness on the way such phenomenon aggregates in financial flows at the macro-level. This approach applied to the United Kingdom and France in Chap. 2 shows that social norms are the channels through which the economic environment of individuals affects their earning opportunities. Adopting such a lens could create an ecological mapping of sustainable earning trends whereby financial flows are broken down horizontally by demographic group, and past, present, and potential future scenarios. It serves the purpose of providing transparency on the extent to which financial accumulation by social groups can hamper or facilitate financial flows towards sectors, occupations, and regions needed to achieve mission-oriented sustainable goals.

In an era of a Triple Planetary Crisis of biodiversity loss, climate change and pollution (UNEP, 2020), with doom prospects for GDP growth, if one accepts methodological groupism where groups can be broadly defined in socio-demographic terms (e.g., occupational, educational, geographical, racial, gender, and so on), it is unlikely that individual earnings will feed into the financial needs of the Great transition without feeding into group biases and associated financial bubbles. In particular, if group behaviour overtakes individual decision-making, it makes us wonder how daily financial decisions, such as personal consumption, savings, investment, as well as education and migration choices can serve the financial needs of the green transition with or without group bias, as seen in Chap. 3. It raises the question of individual versus group legitimacy in financial flows whereby group norms at the level of remembered utility rather than individual instincts at the level of experienced utility serve as a basis for financial exchanges; in which case a financial bubble similar to the one leading to the 2007–2008 crisis is likely to feed into the Great Transition.

Here, the methodological proposition of "groupism" instead of "individualism" is that the legitimacy of financial flows should be first acknowledged to be group-based rather than individual-based. Building on the phenomenon of herd behaviour in decision-making, the following proposition of "sustainable earning trends" is anchored in the rationale that group behaviour has more than a speculative impact on financial flows and serves as a basis for financial capacity-building scenarios to finance the green transition. However, as we have started to explore at the end of Chap. 2, reasoning in terms of "sustainable" trends of earnings means that there is an awareness of these group phenomena at the individual and policy levels. Such awareness would be the first step to move from social-based to ecological-based legitimacy of financial resources, the difference between the two being whether we look at decisions at the point of remembered utility for the former and at the point of experienced utility for the latter.

4.4 Ecological Mapping of the SDGs

The ecological mapping of the SDGs consists of cultivating local islands of excellence in terms of sustainability, where sustainability is understood as the pursuit of life (Dahlmann, 2024). To do so, we need:

1. To map out group biases in local social-ecological systems (Ostrom, 2009) in order to highlight the patterns of sustainable and unsustainable resource use from humans,
2. Locally-based SDGs priorities should be set through community engagement aligned with the Doughnut methodology (Raworth, 2017),
3. To facilitate such islands of excellence, a resilient economic system needs to be in place to protect all the nodes of the system in the event of external shocks. Here, financial systems of protection such as General Average risk management

mechanisms (Fusaro et al., 2023; Demonsant, 2023) combined with Universal Basic Income and other forms of social protection for non-income earners engaged in local resource use and preservation could be used;
4. To financially resource such resilient economic system through local regional, national and international flows targeting the SDGs synergies across the different levels of the SDGs wheels (see Fig. 4.4).

We have seen in Chap. 3 that at the micro-level, Ostrom's rules make it possible to harness the power of group biases to protect common pool resources. At the macro-level however, we have seen that the aggregation of group biases makes it impossible to monitor and control the flow of resources between humans to avoid speculative bubbles or consumption and production bubbles around natural resource use. Applying the lens of group mapping to the SDGs brings transparency and resilience to the economic system impacted by external shocks and resource use. In effect, the core of such a lens is to show how social entitlement rules to resources and financial flows, in particular, can become ecological entitlement rules to a thriving environment. To do so, one needs to understand that top-down financing mechanisms are likely to reinforce existing social entitlement rules to financial resources. Rather, if we are to sustain life on Earth, the ecological footprint of human spending should be maximised towards the pursuit of life.

A way forward in that direction is by nurturing community-based social-ecological systems according to local SDGs priorities. First, the local context is central to the removal of ecologically harmful group biases in decision-making, but only if decisions of all stakeholders are anchored at the level of experienced utility, i.e. the point at which decisions are based on the sensory experiences of the local environment. Otherwise, if decisions are based on remembered utility, then group biases will stay as anchoring point for decision-making and the resulting allocation of resources will sustain existing unequal power relationships and unequal access to resources. Based on the sensory outcomes of experienced utility by local communities (e.g. access to food, green spaces, education, health services, pollution-free air, noise pollution, crime-free environment etc.…), the role of top-down finance is then just to feed into existing community-based narratives of SDG priorities without feeding into harmful group-based practices of financial and non-financial resource accumulation. Second, another important point to focus on the local context, and now promoted in the Global Sustainable Development Report (2023), is that the local context is embedding the indigenous knowledge of the ways in which local social-ecological systems function, which means that indigenous knowledge should be integrated into the local implementation of the SDGs. For example, Fig. 4.3 from Eichberg and Charles (2024) illustrates how the civic university brings the local context and indigenous knowledge into play, enabling to exploit the synergies of the Doughnut (Raworth, 2017) and the SDGs at the local level. The prioritisation of the SDGs aligned with the Doughnut at the local level has also been explored further by Warnecke (2023), showing how the inner ring

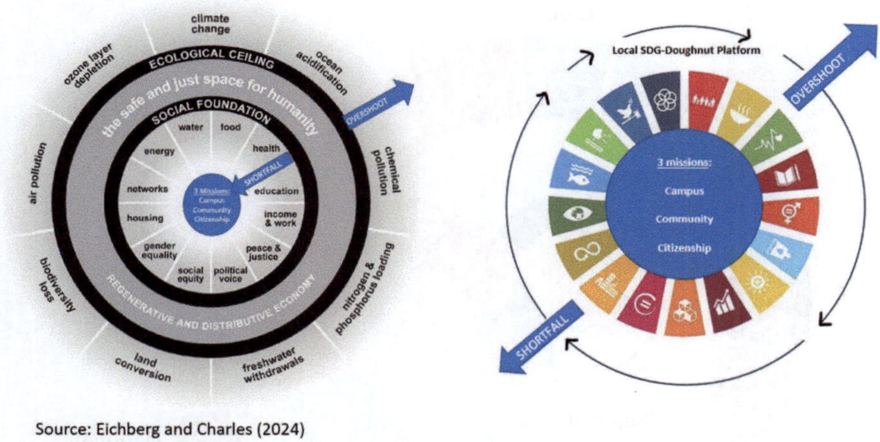

Fig. 4.3 From value-centred missions to a localised SDG platform. Source: Eichberg and Charles (2024)

'Social Foundation' and outer ring 'Ecological Ceiling' components match onto the SDGs and their indicators.

So how do you come about to finance such scheme and create a resilient economic system? Mission-oriented investment led by national and international investment banks and financed by public-private partnerships is certainly one way forward (Mazzucato, 2021, 2023). But how do we make sure that such top-down financial efforts are not taken over by group biases and related green-washing practices? The profit-maximising supply side and the utility-maximising demand side created the perfect combo for the ecological catastrophe of the Great Acceleration, removing the ecological context from decision-making and tapping into group-biases to feed the momentum of financial accumulation, fossil-fuel production, and endless consumption. Adding the group dimension to the SDG framework, from bottom-up, therefore aims at restoring ecological entitlements at the heart of decision-making and rebalancing finance between species to nurture biodiversity, our strongest ally in climate adaptation (UN, 2023).

In a world free from group-biases, Fig. 4.4. provides a schematic example of the ways finance could flow towards local ecological entitlements: looking at the local SDG wheel, we can see that SDG 15 'Life on Land' and SDG 14 'Life below Water' are aligned with their counterparts in the global SDG wheel. With aligned priorities, finance can go straight from global to local biodiversity conservation programmes, on land and below the water, directly through development banks or green bonds, and managed by local shareholders through a SES management structure and General Average (GA) risk management mechanisms for resilience.

Fig. 4.4 Cultivating Islands of SDG excellence from local to regional, national and global SDGs priorities

Box 4.1 General Average Principle and Climate Change as 'Common Peril'

General Average is a principle in maritime law that dates back to ancient times and has been essential in maritime commerce for centuries (Fusaro et al., 2023). It refers to the apportionment of losses resulting from voluntary sacrifices made to save a ship and its cargo during a voyage. This could include actions like throwing cargo overboard to lighten the ship in a storm or cutting away masts to prevent capsizing. Recently, the GA principle has been applied to climate action and systemic resilience (Demonsant, 2023). The GA principle is based on *Voluntary Sacrifice*, when a sacrifice is made for the common safety, such as throwing cargo overboard to lighten the ship during a storm or deliberately grounding a vessel to prevent sinking, it is considered a general average act. Then, all parties involved in the voyage, including the shipowner, cargo owners, and insurers, are required to contribute to cover the losses resulting from the sacrifice. This *contribution* is proportional to the value of their interests that have been saved. A general average adjuster calculates the amount each party must contribute based on the value of the ship, its cargo, and freight. This *calculation* is typically carried out according to the York-Antwerp Rules, a set of standard rules and procedures for determining general average contributions. Once the contributions are determined, the parties involved *settle* their respective shares of the losses. This mechanism was crucial in encouraging cooperation among shipowners, cargo owners, and insurers to ensure the safety of the vessel, its crew, and the cargo. Without it, there might have been less incentive for parties to take necessary actions to save the ship and its cargo during perilous situations. Demonsant (2023) provides a modeling of GA and shows that the action of "common rescue" introduces a key interdependence when the effort of one saves all the others. By considering climate change as a common peril, Demonsant (2023) opens up new perspectives reconciling equity and effectiveness, looking at potential applications in the case of air pollution in cities, where the analysis tends to confirm the positive effects of the rule in relation to Low Emission Zones.

From Fig. 4.4 again, SDG 11 'Sustainable Cities and Communities' is a priority overlapping on both the local and regional SDG wheels where we could see private-public partnerships taking place through job guarantee (Tcherneva, 2020) or universal basic income (Haagh, 2019) programmes, and local subsidies in thriving sectors valuing SDG 11 but also SDG 14 and 15 as stated above in terms of local priorities. Such synergies across levels will also reinforce SDG1 No Poverty which is overlapping on the regional and national SDG wheels. Therefore, at the national level, finance channelled towards addressing poverty needs to account for the synergies with SDG11, SDG14 and SDG15 as previously mentioned, but also the overlapping priorities at the national and global levels of SDG3 'Good Health and Well-being', and SDG4 'Quality Education'. Using the SDGs wheels as compass for policy priorities at different levels does have its synergies and trade-offs, a persistent argument on the SDG framework (Dawes, 2019). However, starting from the bottom-up allows to anchor the ecological ceiling and social foundations of the Doughnut at the local level.

The SDGs as mode of governance from the local to the global levels will give more legitimacy and accountability to the Agenda 2023, which is currently missing at the local level and across many countries. The institutionalization of the SDGs is one of the four recommendations put forward by Biermann et al. (2023) which, half-way through its implementation, is key to accelerating the Agenda 2030. Legitimacy and accountability would also help cross-fertilizing finance as exemplified schematically above, by using a set of financial instruments and mechanisms across the SDGs and at various levels, from local to global. In the current state of resource flows with group biases and looking at the bubbling effect affecting the resilience of the entire system of financial flows in Fig. 4.1, the largest node could be representing SDG 12 'Responsible Consumption and Production' which, under current business-as-usual trends lead resources, from natural to financial, to feed into that bubble. Meanwhile, SDG14 'Life Below Water' is one of the most important ecological leverage point to mitigate climate change (Charles & Blondel, 2023), yet it is also one of the most underfunded SDGs by both Official Development

Assistance and philanthropic development funding (OECD, 2020). In Fig. 4.1, it could be representing one of the under-financed nodes adjacent to largest one representing SDG14. Whether improving the fluidity and resilience of the entire system of financial flows in Fig. 4.2 occur would depend on taking ‘groupism’ rather than ‘individualism’ seriously in policy-making.

4.5 Conclusion

Building resilient economic systems at the national and international levels with a group perspective can inform policy-making of the potential cognitive biases at the individual level, which aggregate at the macro-level to create unhealthy bubbles of resource accumulation. Adopting such a lens could inform sustainable earning trends whereby financial flows by group can hamper or facilitate financial flows towards sectors, occupations, and regions prone to herd behaviour. What makes an economic system resilient? It is one that first recognises the role of group behaviour in financial accumulation and manages to redirect its excesses where needed. This Chapter therefore looked at the bubbling effect of group accumulation affecting the resilience of the entire system of financial flows, before describing how to improve the fluidity and resilience of the system. Then, adding the group dimension to the SDG framework, from bottom-up, aimed at restoring ecological entitlements at the heart of decision-making and rebalancing finance between species to nurture biodiversity. Linking international and national finance to local initiatives without greenwashing effects requires improving the fluidity and resilience of the entire system of financial flows occur would depend on taking ‘groupism’ rather than ‘individualism’ seriously in policy-making. Ironically enough, it is also an individual task for each of us to go back to the point of experienced utility in decision-making: sensing the ecological context of decision-making to trigger the individual responsibility of one’s ecological footprint.

References

Biermann, F., Sun, Y., Banik, D., Beisheim, M., Bloomfield, M. J., Charles, A., Chasek, P., Hickmann, T., Pradhan, P., & Sénit, C.-A. (2023). Four governance reforms to strengthen the SDGs: A demanding policy vision can accelerate global sustainable development efforts. *Science, 381*(6663), 1159–1160. https://doi.org/10.1126/science.adj5434

Bonizzi, B., & Kaltenbrunner, A. (2024). International financial subordination in the age of asset manager capitalism. *Environment and Planning A: Economy and Space*. https://doi.org/10.1177/0308518X241227744

Charles, A., & Blondel, P. (Eds.). (2023). Our oceans: A deep dive. *Institute for Policy Research Report*. https://doi.org/10.5281/zenodo.7736214

Dahlmann, F. (2024). Conceptualising sustainability as the pursuit of life. *Journal of Business Ethics*. https://doi.org/10.1007/s10551-024-05617-y

Dawes, J. (2019). Are the sustainable development goals self-consistent and mutually achievable? *Sustainable Development, 28*, 101–117. https://doi.org/10.1002/sd.1975

Demonsant, C. (2023). L'atténuation du changement climatique à l'épreuve de l'équité : Étude de la règle des avaries communes et de ses implications pour l'action climatique. Gestion et management. Université Paris sciences et lettres, 2023. Français. NNT : 2023UPSLM039ff. tel-04318240f.

Eichberg, E., & Charles, A. (2024). The role of the civic university in facilitating inclusive and transformative pedagogical approaches to the sustainable development goals: A systematic literature review. *Sustainability, 16*(7). https://doi.org/10.3390/su16072752

Fusaro, M., Addobbati, A., & Piccinno, L. (2023). *General average and risk management in medieval and early modern maritime business*. Palgrave Macmillan. https://doi.org/10.1007/978-3-031-04118-1

Gibadullina, A. (2023). *Who owns and controls global capital? Uneven geographies of asset manager capitalism*. Economy and Space. https://doi.org/10.1177/0308518X231195890

Global Sustainable Development Report (GSDR). (2023). *Times of crisis, times of change: Science for accelerating transformations to sustainable developmen*t. Independent Group of Scientists appointed by the Secretary-General, United Nations, New York.

Guariso, D., Castañeda, G., & Guerrero, O. A. (2023). Budgeting for SDGs: Quantitative methods to assess the potential impacts of public expenditure. *Development Engineering, 8*. https://doi.org/10.1016/j.deveng.2023.100113

Haagh, L. (2019). *The case for universal basic income*. Polity.

ILO. (2022). *Global wage report 2022–23: The impact of inflation and COVID-19 on wages and purchasing power*. International Labour Office.

Mazzucato, M. (2021). *Mission economy: A moonshot guide to changing capitalism, Allen Page*. Penguin Book.

Mazzucato, M. (2023). Financing the sustainable development goals through mission-oriented development banks. UN DESA Policy Brief Special issue. UN Department of Economic and Social Affairs; UN High-level Advisory Board on Economic and Social Affairs; University College London Institute for Innovation and Public Purpose. September.

Nesbitt-Ahmed, Z. (2023). *How gender-responsive age-sensitive social protection is related to the climate crisis: A summary of the evidence*. Innocenti Research Report, UNICEF Innocenti—Global Office of Research and Foresight.

OECD. (2020). SDG 14 is among the least funded SDGs by both official development assistance and philanthropic development funding: Normalised 2017 commitments. In *Sustainable Ocean for all: Harnessing the benefits of Sustainable Ocean economies for developing countries*. The development dimension. OECD Publishing. https://doi.org/10.1787/202afb81-en

Ostrom, E. (1990). *Governing the commons: The evolution of institutions for collective action*. Cambridge University Press.

Ostrom, E. (2009). A General framework for analyzing sustainability of social-ecological systems. *Science, 325*(5939), 419–422. https://doi.org/10.1126/science.1172133

Raworth, K. (2017). *Doughnut economics: Seven ways to think like a 21st-century economist*. Chelsea Green Publishing.

Tcherneva, P. R. (2020). The case for a job guarantee. *Polity*.

United Nations. (2023). *Biodiversity – our strongest natural defense against climate change*. Retrieved 2024-03-07, from https://www.un.org/en/climatechange/science/climate-issues/biodiversity

United Nations Environment Programme. (2020). *The triple planetary crisis: Forging a new relationship between people and the earth*. UNEP. 2020-07-14. Retrieved 2024-03-06.

Warnecke, T. (2023). Operationalizing the doughnut economy: An institutional perspective. *Journal of Economic Issues, 57*, 643–653.

Correction to: Sustainable Earnings in a Resilient Economic System

Correction to:

A. Charles, *Sustainable Earnings in a Resilient Economic System*, SpringerBriefs in Economics, https://doi.org/10.1007/978-3-031-67573-7

The original version of the book was inadvertently published with incorrect copyright holder in the front matter. This has been corrected.

The updated version of this book can be found at
https://doi.org/10.1007/978-3-031-67573-7

A. Charles, *Sustainable Earnings in a Resilient Economic System*,
SpringerBriefs in Economics, https://doi.org/10.1007/978-3-031-67573-7_5

MIX
Papier aus verantwortungsvollen Quellen
Paper from responsible sources
FSC® C105338

If you have any concerns about our products,
you can contact us on
ProductSafety@springernature.com

In case Publisher is established outside the EU,
the EU authorized representative is:
Springer Nature Customer Service Center GmbH
Europaplatz 3, 69115 Heidelberg, Germany

Printed by Libri Plureos GmbH
in Hamburg, Germany